Last Waltz of the Tyrants

THE PROPHECY

Edited by
JUDI POPE KOTEEN

Published by
Beyond Words Publishing, Inc.
Pumpkin Ridge Road
Route 3, Box 492-B
Hillsboro, OR 97123
Phone: 503-647-5109
Toll Free: 1-800-284-9673

DISCLAIMER
This book is designed to provide information in regard to the subject matter covered. The purpose of this book is to educate and entertain. The author, editors, and publisher shall have neither liability nor responsibility to any person or entity with respect to any loss or damage caused, directly or indirectly, by the information contained in this book.

Printed in the United States of America
by Arcata Graphics, Kingsport, Tennessee

Library of Congress Catalog Card Number: 88-070821
ISBN: 0-941831-26-4

Special thanks to Jenni and Adrianne
my little lights

To all who desire to know

Foreword

IN 1977, RAMTHA appeared before JZ Knight in the doorway of her kitchen in Tacoma, Washington. Nothing has been the same since.

Ramtha is an enigma. He calls himself such. And without a doubt, as the focus of society moves beyond the phenomenon of channeling and more people begin to take a serious look at the message, Ramtha will be hailed as one of the greatest communicators and teachers of all time.

He lived on Earth 35,000 years ago and for the better part of that life was a savage conqueror, until he was wounded in a battle. He withdrew to a mountain to contemplate life and spent seven years upon a barren rock, considering the sun and moon, and life and death, and things that never seem to change. And when he left that rock and returned to his waiting army, he returned an enlightened being, for he had seen through the illusion called life. He stayed and taught his people for many years and ultimately ascended before thousands. He is "The Ram" around which the Hindu people built their religion.

He describes himself as part of a brotherhood of beings who love humankind greatly, who have come with information to help us make the choices necessary in order for us to gain personal sovereignty in the days to come. His is an enabling message, an empowering message.

Once, when asked what he would say if he could reach the whole world with a single most important message, he said, "I would tell you that you are God and that you are greatly loved."

Books created from Ramtha's words are based on weekend

events called Intensives, where he speaks extemporaneously about a given subject. Ramtha has spoken about upcoming world changes previously.

The foretellings in this book were delivered during a period of time that is no longer. For time, as we call it, is ever moving. Ramtha is very clear about the predictions in this book. He says they are "as it is seen now." He made these predictions in November, 1987. Humankind has free will, and we can change our minds. Much of what is forecast here is based on human choice, as it was seen then. Ramtha speaks here of the effect of collective consciousness and says that the light is being pressed to many now. A shift in collective consciousness can change many things that are foretold here, yet Ramtha says some of the things cannot be changed, like the Earth's need to replenish itself. Given the above, we encourage the reader not to be as concerned about the prediction as with the understanding behind the prediction.

The Afterword includes a listing of other Ramtha titles. We recommend that you read them to gain a full understanding of the breadth of Ramtha's message.

Table of Contents

THE PROPHECY

PART I

The Window
of Understanding

T HE MESSAGE YOUR EYES deliver to you here is liken unto a window where the coverlets have been drawn back so that you may see the distant horizon that awaits. This message is for you, when you walk into the light of your new day, to help you to know where you are going. Very few of you have known where you were going — your life was simply a matter of living in a state of social consciousness and saying, "Alas, this is all there is." What is social consciousness? Living for others who won't die for you; earning for others who won't loan you a penny; loving others who don't know what love is.

Many eyes will scan these pages . . . I salute you. For, though certainly in this time you did not have to march over long distances for a sortie and thus earn the right to read this, nor did you have to beg permission from your liege to scan these pages, you have, in your own way, earned the right to see this information. I'm very pleased also in addressing you, to see where your voyages have taken you to bring you to this book at this time.

I wish to tell you something about these moments in time we are about to spend together. These words are not revealed to you to encourage fear, trepidation, sorrow, and despair. Yet, it will take great courage to read these words. These communiqués were not created as a conspiracy against you or to create fear in the marketplace, nor are they given to *own* you.

This message is not for a bunch of spiritualistic airy fairies who

1

clamor that their way is the *only* way. This message is business: the business of survival. This is certainly not a message for anyone who hides behind spiritual cloaks wandering around in twentieth-century monasteries, lacking the courage to live in the real world.

This message is for the mature in spirit. It is an understanding that is applicable to your bare existence. This is certainly not a message for you to play children's games with, for those hours are finished. So I am very pleased to see not only that you have the courage to read this, but that you desire the opportunity — acquired through having knowledge of the Now and of the future — to *choose* to make the proper decisions that are important to the gift that you have, the gift called Life.

Courage is really immanent within the God that created you. There is the *within* you, the ego; and there is the *without* you, the altered ego. The altered ego lacks courage; it only snivels excuses. That you are ready to read these words says a grand amount about you. Your open willingness to grow thusly sings in the winds of forever about where you've come from and where you're going.

You won't remember everything that you will read here because you will have a tendency to fog out what you do not want to hear. But, unlike watching your television box, you can pick this book up and reread and reread and reread, if you so desire.

What is a *fog out?* That's the altered ego filtering out what is conducive to the inner being. In other words, you hear what you want to hear; you see what you want to see; you read what you want to read. So, inevitably, you will have memory lapses. Most of you who read this will hear it all and will understand it all. You will have a clear vision as to what is coming, not only to this plane, but inevitably to your own small, intimate world.

The words appearing on these pages have been placed here by a writer taking what I have spoken and translating it to the page. What the words are, though, is only verbiage. And certainly my verbiage has been criticized. But what you hear me say is simply a reflection of you and what you understand. The verbiage is only there to impart realities. Words cripple emotions desperately, but the words given in this book have a living fire all their own.

And those entities that are intertwined with destiny will have a revelation that will come into being from reading these words. Why? Because the words simply evoke the inward vision to see what heretofore you have not seen.

There is much more occurring than can be put into words. There are many levels involved in this demonstrative level called life. And many of those levels are beyond words. They cannot be uttered. And if they could, you would not understand them. So in this time that we spend together, you will read words that will allow you to understand the changes afoot and your right to make choices within them. They will be even, fair words spread out before you in even doses, paragraph by paragraph. Nothing will be held back that can be shared. Your reaction to what you read here will be seen in the choices you make in the next few months and years.

Free Will Is What Sets You Apart from the Angels

Now, masters: choice. It is very important for you to understand the concept of choice, for choice is an inalienable right that every entity possesses. You are endowed by the creator with free will. *Free will* is the ability to choose, and from that choice to instigate co-creation with the eternal IS . . . the Mother/Father principle . . . God Almighty . . . the All that is the All.

Free will. That is what sets you apart from what you call angels, for you embody that which is termed the mystery of all other life forms. Free will, choice, and a soul have been breathed into what you are, to allow you to evolve through the processes called life.

Choice. Everything that you choose to do, you do. And that instrument is called choice within the soul. Everyone has access to these words, and yet the knowledge is only given to you so that you then can react according to your own choices. That is your endowment from God . . . the Father/Mother principle that is within you — your right to choose. It is one of the greatest gifts you have, and when you lose freedom and liberty you have lost the right to choose. So up until this point in your time, as it is so termed, you have been able to activate the concept of choice. You do not have to believe or accept what you read here. You can say, "It is of no truth to me." And it will not be. You can choose to say, "This is non-existent," and it won't exist for you. And yet, you are still loved; you are still important, regardless of your choice. You will read these things and act according to your choice in your reality. You will choose to react according to where you are in your growth. Choices allow you to evolve . . . to bring evolution home where it belongs. Or you may choose to stay stuck in your past, where many of you have been wallowing. It is your choice.

What is given here may not agree with your own concise truth. You may not allow it to agree, and still that is by choice as well. But I desire for you to know that it is not forced upon you to hear, to do, or to react to anything that is revealed to you here. And if your neighbors are running amuck and telling you, "You had best do this or you're going to be sorry," it still comes down to *your* choice. Use it in everything that you see here. You *chose* to read this book; thus you have earned the right to see what is written. This book will only communicate to you what your eyes are ready to see. You will only absorb what you are ready to absorb, only accept what you are ready to accept.

Fear Keeps the Guardian at the Door, and the Guardian Is the Altered Ego

You also have the choice of whether to be afraid of what you read here. And fear is what keeps the guardian at the door. The altered ego is the guardian that stands at the door of your soul, keeping you in a holding pattern in your life, only allowing in what it filters. Imagine the great ego breathed into you by the IS. Then imagine it altered by a mysterious force that keeps you from yourself. You can choose to fear or to learn; you can choose to advance according to the knowledge or be weakened by it. You can choose to utilize it in your life or discard it. But though you are flesh and blood — and most tenuous you are, for your feelings can get hurt easily, just as a slight tear within the tissue causes you to bleed — you are nonetheless divine. You are a human glory of God — not less than, but *part* of, a human *glory* of, brethren and sisteren to God you are.

It is up to you what you do with what I say here, for what is given is knowledge as it is seen. The living word will manifest, for the living word is already in the throes of manifestation. Many of these things you will hear are already in the process of happening, and many are yet to unfold from that happening.

Now, *time*. Time is, in essence, an illusion. Those who do not perceive the unseen world are, in essence, hypocrites because they worship time. They live by what is called a clock, whether it is a water clock, a sand clock, or a mechanical clock, and *time* is unseen. Time, because it is illusionary, is not an absolute truth. Because the illusion fluctuates according to those who create the illusion.

What I say unto you here is seen in this moment, as it is now. Many of you ask, "How many days do I have?" "Should I do this today?" "Should I have done it yesterday?" "Do I have enough beans yet?" What will be imparted to you will be based as closely on your time frame as you feel you need it to be. And what I say will be seen and calculated from *this moment*. Everything that exists *now* is a product of a creative force yesterday; of thoughts, of attitudes, of wishes, desires, and indeed choices. Did you read that? Everything is a product of a creative force *yesterday!* Yesterday you imagined that today would be here, and here it is! All of you *knew* today would be here and so it is for all of you. Those who couldn't imagine it aren't here to enjoy it.

Manifested destiny is your life as you have created it, the way you are living, what you have created, which is where you are. Manifested destiny in regards to the human drama, indeed the human element, is made manifest in your lives according to the choices you make based on the collective attitude that you have.

So if you are stuck in your altered ego, and your life is nothing but a swift repetition of yesterday, then you, by choice, are living with a repetitious attitude which keeps creating the same tomorrow.

Tomorrow Has to Come; You Have Too Many Appointments

Tomorrow — can you prove that tomorrow is coming? Can you prove that a fortnight from now is coming, except by your calendars? It *has* to come; you have too many appointments for it not to. You are counting on two weeks from now to happen — get it? That is how you *know* two weeks from now is coming. But as of this moment, it is unprovable that it exists.

Now, two weeks from this day in your life, your intimate destiny will manifest according to your emotional attitudes gleaned this day; for your lives will change in a fortnight according to what you have gained in knowledge this day. It *will* manifest because when you broaden your reality, and indeed broaden your perception, your manifested destiny broadens as well. What you read here this day can effect your tomorrow if you send the message to your soul to remove the guardian from the door.

Human beings are very fickle. Indeed — you are slippery creatures. Yes, you are. The rules of karma, eternal sin, and all of those things of limited teaching *belong* to limited understanding because, when you engage choice, at any moment you can *change your mind;* thus you change your destiny. Your destiny is changed automatically because destiny is the *moment* where you mind is, the *now,* as it is seen *now.* And if you wake up in the morn and change your whole attitude — when you are no longer a sniveling scaredy cat and you wake up brave as a bear with a new innate knowingness — your *now,* your destiny, will change. You are very flexible; your lives are very flexible and it's all based on choice. Choice. Isn't it grander to love than to hate? Isn't it grander to forgive than to war? It's all choice.

Consider this now. Look at where you are this very moment, sitting there, lying there. This *now,* this very moment in time, is a result of a fortnight ago in the past. You programmed it. It has come together; that is what created this moment. Humanity, as a whole, works on the same principle. You're no different than your brothers who are living in space. They are doing *their thing,* as it is so termed. You are the *same* as they are. So the destiny of the human race is indeed a *manifested* destiny based on the collective attitude of individual human beings. And as it is seen this moment, destiny is manifesting in the time flow according to the attitude right *now.*

How can you talk about the future? To specify days and moments is arduous. To talk about the future of humanity is simple — because the collective attitude produces manifested destiny in everyone's life.

In this passage I am going to tell you about the human drama — man's destruction of man and nature. The things that are seen in the human drama that are outside of the window of your view are based entirely upon the collective movement of humanity at this moment. It is based on what the goals of humanity are at this *very* moment. And those goals, as they are seen at this moment, are on their way to manifestation. Remember, what you feel this day and embrace is the law — it *must* manifest, get it?

The Guardian Keeps You from Evolving

The predictability of your beloved brethren, humanity, is simple. Though you have the opportunity to change at any moment, for the most part the only thing in this ever-changing universe which moves eternally forward that has not changed is the human being. Nature is the splendor of God evolving, ever changing, ever moving forward, never achieving perfection, for what you term perfection is a limitation. And yet, in this ever-evolving universe, there is one species that refuses to evolve; and it does so because of fear. And that is the human being.

In this book, we will address the predictability and the manifested destiny of human beings as a whole. This more intimately affects who you are because the manifested destiny will radically change your lifestyle. It is supposed to. Nature, through evolution, is set in a forward motion called *forever.* That movement is easily determined, for nature moves forward in spite of the stagnation of the human being.

But let us address you and your brethren so you can understand why what I call *Changes: The Days to Come* are coming more rapidly, and why they will have such a profound affect on who and what you are; and yes, on where you live and where you labor. This understanding, remember, is knowledge. Listen to it. Choose to understand, because when you can see out of the window, you can change the direction of your path and survive it all.

Survival is a very important subject here because, in the days to come, it will be imperative for you to be on your own path, moving forward in alignment with nature; thus you will survive many things coming. And you will learn about all of those changes in the time it takes you to read this book. The knowledge of this information allows you the opportunity to survive everything. It also gives you enlightenment and takes you out of the superstitious fear and dogma that has kept you in ignorance. Those who will survive all things that are coming are those who are enhanced with knowledge. So let us begin.

A Shadow Falls
on the World

IN THE SPACES BETWEEN other words, I've talked a lot about man/ woman and the creation of the altered ago. The reason that humanity is stuck in its repetitious pattern is that you have created the altered ego. The altered ego is indeed the Antichrist; it is indeed referred to as the wickedness of man; it is indeed the familiar pattern through which *all* peoples have lived, since even my times. It has become the image, the identity. And the image and identity are hungry beasts that must always be fed.

When you live through your altered ego, you divide the strength of your divinity. It takes part of your divinity to keep up the power of keeping up a good face, doing all the right things, saying all the right things, living *all* the right ways. It takes energy, your life force, to keep up the layers. And yet, the divinity that is suppressed is the great ego, which is the God Within. *That* is the stagnation of the soul that has not evolved for 35,000 years. It has all gone to keep up the image. Aren't you tired yet?

Now, image: when one lives for image, there are certain things one must do to keep the image alive and well. Until recently, man thought he had to do certain things to become a man. And woman feared she could only survive by doing certain things, so that her survival would be assured through *man*kind. And as you grow to understand the evolution of the soul, you will readily understand the altered ego and its place, even on this day.

Now, we're going to speak here of *man* — the male gender.

The *male* gender, in the thrust of change, is responsible for what is occurring in your world economically. He is responsible for what is occurring in your world with regards to famine. The male gender is responsible for what is occurring in your world with regards to war. We are going to talk about man — *men.*

In creating the division from women, it was necessary, eons ago, for a man not to have an association with a woman, because God, after all, was a man. His *son* was a man, and it has been suggested that the *Holy Ghost,* whatever that is, was a man! To male understanding, the man was ultimately divine and woman merely there to serve. Consequently, she could only obtain divinity through the pleading of her husband-man to God on her behalf. In man, a distinct characterization began to emerge when women came to be considered soulless, many ages ago. Man, for fear of reflection, had to take on certain emotional capacities that would allow him an *exalting* of self while he maintained a separateness from his women. And all of those emotions that make up your *image* are suppressed in the body today.

Now, the image is what we are going to be talking about here. A man could not weep. He could not show compassion or tenderness. He could not shed a tear in a sweet moment, nor stop to feel the silken petal of a wildflower. For if he did so, he would be considered weak and therefore considered a woman, who we all know was not considered divine. The man had to be an achiever, had to be a *winner,* could not be a failure; failure was indicative of women. Man began to determine that it was his duty not only to impregnate the world, but to see to its other affairs. Thus man began to devise and create an image in which lust for self-achievement was the ultimate power; that was what he worked for, desired, coveted. When man slept, his sweet dreams were not of lilacs and small children. His dreams were of conquering other men and being seen as powerful in their eyes.

Now, though this has gone on for 35,000 years in your counting, every *single* lifetime, every *generation,* cements the division of men and women and their images. Even your teachings of God through what is called religion have separated men from women, even while they pray. Man's ultimate achievement was not to *love,* according to this created image; his ultimate achievement was to have power, for that power empowered his image and gave him credibility.

Where woman's ultimate achievement would be to have her perfect man love her, her perfect man's ultimate achievement according to his image would be business and power, not loving a woman. So now you understand why men took lightly their *affairs,* as we shall term them — fornicating, rolling in the hay. Do you understand? That meant nothing to them; it only represented sexual gratification and release.

Now, as your centuries began to wind on, this image became more and more powerful. It was *man* who was the King and, indeed, it was *man* who was the warrior. It was man who was the conqueror; men were always creating wars with one another, often using the excuse of *it is God's will* so they could appease this altered ego, this great image that they *had to* live up to. Every lifetime the goal of that soul would be to achieve power; it wasn't love — love does not sit well in the altered ego. Love rests in the God Within, the ego; not in the image of the ego; not in the image that overlays all of you reading this book.

Soon They Forget You Did Anything at the Circuses

Power. If you become a conqueror and conquer another conqueror you have power, yes? But it's so fleeting because the masses are fickle and soon they forget that you did anything at the circuses. So you *must* go out and conquer some more. And you have to keep it up to glorify yourself. And that glorification, remember, is suppressed by image. The natural glory which is within is suppressed by the altered ego, so you never even get to *feel* the glory. So you have to keep it up even harder!

Do you know that your altered ego stands as a guardian to your soul, your subconscious? It does not allow anything that does not fit its image to be seated in the soul. In other words, suppose someone says you are loved. Your altered ego would say, "Get outta here," and that feeling would never reach the soul to become known. In every lifetime the altered ego only lets into the soul what fits its image; that's why you've been in a rut for so long. Back to the men. These men continued to battle. The victors formed tribes, then governments and kingdoms to govern the people, often in the name of God, *their* god, whichever god that was. Thus began the terror of country conquering country and the human misery, slaughter and stench that has continued for 35,000 years.

What was important to the conqueror? That he ransack his victim's treasury — you know, loot it; that proved he had won. That's why you will find ancient treasures scattered all over the world, displayed with such pride. Precious ancient artifacts are sitting in mausoleums; they are the centerpieces of driveways and roads with grass down the middle. And you look upon them with great pride — "Yes, yes, yes, this was Cleopatra's knitting needle," or whatever it was called, and everyone says, "Oh, isn't that wonderful! It is brilliant! It is a work of art!" and no one asks, "How did we acquire it?"

Thus the acquisition of stolen treasuries became *revered* as an accomplishment. Are you aware that the display of the loot of an owned, *conquered* kingdom is still revered today? And the looters are very self-righteous — they went to war, they conquered, they owned. "I came. I saw. I conquered!" — a triad spoken throughout man's existence. It is considered nothing to assail a dead king's tomb, taking his treasures for the sake of history; and it is considered nothing to assail a kingdom and to put its peoples to the yoke. Whether the spoils of war were the treasures of the conquered nation or the enslavement of their peoples, robbery was legitimized by your ancestors.

This conquering and plundering went on for quite a while. Therefore, all the kings always possessed the bullion stores and the human resources needed to take on any march, to take any stand — they were *very* wealthy. The conqueror took from the conquered their land, and in the process they tore down forests and planted grains. They raped the land. They took the product of the land and sent it to their own country to feed their hoards and the mobs in the marketplace. Politicians had to keep the mobs happy, don't you know? They had to keep their bellies filled, had to keep entertainment in front of them. Why? Because it was important to have votes when that came into style; it is the *people* who keep their kings in power.

What happened to the lands of some of these exotic countries that you don't even remember, land that was once covered by ancient forests and ripe with pungent, sweet grasses? What happened to their glittering treasures, mined carefully so as not to disturb the earth? They were *ravaged* by conquering kings over time. And all that is left now are areas that look like deserts, dust bowls, *wastelands* where once thrived succulent forests and nocturnal creatures of mystery. Now there is just dust — not very mysterious at all.

The French Lesson

This segment of history went on for quite a while until there entered into the drama a wondrous entity called Napoleon. Have you heard of him, aye? Well, prior to him were all the Caesars. To a Caesar, it wasn't really necessary to go out and locate financing for a march — they simply marched and took it. And then came this great conqueror with dreams of glory, dreams of resurrecting his country to be preeminent in his world in those days. And yet his country was bankrupt, because the peoples, the mobs if you will, had overthrown the aristocracy. You know: chop, *chop,* CHOP? And as a result they got rid of all noble blood existing in the country at that time, because they blamed the noblemen for their intense poverty. And they were right.

So the conqueror comes to lift his beloved country out of the gutter, to make it preeminent in its ancient place. And along comes a dallying individual who sees that he can make a tidy return on this undertaking. He finances Napoleon and his marches, gives him a substantial loan to go out and conquer, and whatever loot Napoleon brings back he can use to repay the debt. Are you with me? Yes. Now remember, women stayed home and men were doing the marching (and a few weaklings stayed behind and took care of the women).

They Are Called Graymen

And thus was born, with Napoleon's first conquest, what you will read about in the rest of this book. They are called Graymen. The entity that Napoleon secured the gold from created a wonderful system of supplying and financing conquests. It turned out to be a *very* lucrative business with a very nice return, a business that is about to alter the face of the world as you know it. One important idea occurred to this early financier. He realized that in order to be successful at this business, he could not swear allegiance to *any* country. His business began to spread. To be the entrepreneur, setting up financing for anyone who wanted to play war, he realized it was important not to have allegiance to any country, but simply to be there to fulfill the need.

This particular *first* Grayman had no woman that he cared for and loved. But he had sons. They were a treasure, for they meant that his divine heritage would go on. And it did. This man saw an image of achievement in his altered ego of *ultimate* wealth. Now, listen — no one wants money for its own sake, but rather for what it can do. And to the image of this beginning Grayman, obtaining wealth was the key that unlocked the door to power. It wasn't money; it was *power* that fulfilled this need, this image.

This wonderful Grayman quickly realized, upon a *large* return on his investment, that he could work both sides against the middle, and he did. He helped a country called Austria and a country called Poland.

Soon this man and his sons were collecting a nice, orderly return off everyone involved in a conflict. And they found it to their benefit to *generate* conflicts. Are you with me? Yes, the lights are going on somewhat. The more they could encourage conflicts and feed the altered egos of lusty kings and lusty conquerors, the more they profited and the more powerful they became.

One of the side benefits of this power was the created ability to put their sons and the people they owned into very influential offices. In other words, if the king said, "No, I'm giving that position to my third cousin twice removed," then this nice, tidy little Grayperson would say to him, "Well, how unfortunate that is, because I really felt that the individual I'm recommending would do a splendid job, and since that can't come to pass, then I really *must* ask you to pay me everything you owe me, as soon as you can, of course." And, of course, the king would return to his castle, bite his nails, chew on them, curse, gnash his teeth and come back with, "Oh, I would love to have your person fill this office."

The Shadow Is Cast

Since Napoleon's time, the influence of the Graymen has grown immeasurably, yet they have retained the power personally and within their direct-lineage families. They began to set up banks. They began to influence governments. They began to influence the kings and leaders of those governments. And those who didn't play ball with the Graymen had their gold supply cut off, and they found themselves cut off from countries they'd had open relationships with before. In the great whore that was called Europa, everything was being dictated through the power of gold and the paper that it was written on.

After the turn of the nineteenth century (or the 1800s, as they are called), a great man who was the inheritor of these beginning Graymen activities inherited this wonderful business plan. It continued in his hands and in his family; and those who were chosen to work with him began to control Europa.

Every war since the first Napoleon has been manipulated, set up, and financed by the Graymen and their families. And if the inkling of war didn't exist, they created it. At any cost. Remember, these gray families had no allegiance to any country. Therefore, they had no allegiance to any country's laws and no allegiance to any religious belief. They were on their own, which allowed them to carry out their enterprises quite nicely. They created dictators out of common people, feeding them through their altered ego. They created assassinations. They created blame, outbreaks, and dissension, all for power. Money, yes, but the money bought them the power, because every man had his price and every kingdom certainly had its price. Are you with me? You've seen this drama played on the stage before?

The name of this man from the 1800s was Rothschild; hear you that name? Remember it, because very soon you will begin to see how a further crumbling in the equality of human beings all over the world was directed by this family.

In the year 1857, this dynasty had persons who were in allegiance with them placed in important positions, in decision-making positions, throughout Europe. They had them in place in other countries around the world. And they were beginning to place them in America.

In 1857, there was a meeting in London. There they plotted all the wars that would occur in Europa and in the Americas, up to the last war plotted, which was World War II; yes, as recently as that time.

These families are also the same individuals that created the war between the Northern and Southern peoples of America. The families, in coalition with munitions makers who *also* had no allegiance to any one country, created the civil outbreak that occurred in America. The battlefields were manipulated; the North wanted the wealth of the South. The enslavement of the human being was not the reason for the scourge, but merely an excuse for it. The slaves were already in the process of receiving their freedom, long before this outbreak occurred. The war was contrived to gain control of Southern wealth.

Lincoln was a great king, I wish you to know. There has not been another like him. This individual had endeavored since his election to stop buying money from Europe, purely for economic purposes. He also knew all about the conflict that was being created, pitting brother against brother. He *desperately* endeavored to enact for his country — for its people — a system whereby

America would own its *own* money rather than buying it from Europe. And when he had made the decision for his country to print its own money, for the sovereignty of its people, *without* interest, he was done away with. Simple enough — he posed a threat to an already enrooted system in Europa, a system that, at present, was controlling the economies of the world and certainly the economy of this new and raw nation. It wasn't a madman who destroyed this wonderful man; it was a hired assassin. Consequently, money continued to flow to America, supported by outside interests.

Now, to bring you presently to the first world war. They called it the Great War. An interesting name for a war: the *great* war. This war was created and financed by not only the bankers in this country, but the bankers in England and in Switzerland. It was created to bring about the often-proposed taxation system which the Graymen desired to put squarely on the shoulders of the American people. The war was created to get you *involved*. It was created to bring Europa under submission. It was created to further instill their money control in this country, and so it went about as planned.

Remember, the banks in America and in England, and indeed in other countries worldwide, supported this war. The Americans at this time were just discovering freedom and opportunity and land. And yes, there were hard times, but they had one grand thing that caused them to leave Europa in the first place — *freedom!* They could worship as they believed, they could live as they chose to live, and they were not under the suppression of tyrants from their homeland. America was not made up of one specific creed of people; it was the melting pot of the world, so to speak. *Freedom* — and everyone was enjoying that freedom *immensely* in America.

I want you to know that America had just gotten out of a horrible war with Cuba. Ever hear of that? Well, you know about Rough Riding Ted. Let me tell you, Cuba was once a great island, a grand people. They were not revolutionists; they were meek *farmers.* They had no revolutionary designs, and yet your country, through propaganda, was taught about the *enemy below them*, and the *threat to world peace* this small country of farmers posed. Farmers? The munitions people had a hand in that; they're the ones who created the war and *imported* the disputers and revolutionists. And so this country went to war to wipe out the Cuban insurgents. Do you know who they slaughtered? Farmers who didn't know what the big deal was about, who had never thought about a war. They had only thought about their harvest, their children, their love of God, their belief in their Church. They had harmed no one, but they were the *insurgents* and had to be done away with. That war was created by the Graymen.

It took a lot to get this country into the first world war, because no one wanted to get into it. And so the Graymen, owning most of the media . . . do you know what the media is? I have learned that term! The Graymen own them *all;* you know, the papers you read, the box you watch, the magazines you thumb through, the radio waves you listen to. Because it was important to have control of what you read, see and hear. They told the papers what to print and what not to print. Well, they went on and on and on, in a media campaign about this war, about the patriotism of this country. And those who did not help wave the banner of liberty were considered traitors. You were manipulated quite handily!

There was a very hot political campaign that went on in your country to ensure that you got involved. Do you remember what finally immersed you into that little pickle? What was the incident? Bully for you — yes, a sinking ship. Listen, did you know that passenger ships leaving the shores of your continent were carrying contraband? They were carrying war supplies even before you got involved. So you got into it. And how brave of all your sons and, yes, some of your daughters to die in that war! It was a war for liberty, to create freedom, and to save Europe from the menace of Germany! What a lark! It wasn't that at all! It was a propagandized manipulation.

And when it was over with, this country had borrowed

enormously to support its war debt. Therefore, it was subtly suggested that the way to repay the loan would be to again tax the people. So, the tax was passed. The people were paying taxes to pay off their loan from the Graymen, who finally were receiving a return on their investment. But the Graymen wanted the taxes to go on . . . and on, and on and *on,* because they wanted you to be indebted to them as the people in Europa already were.

A lot went on in this time in your history. Your media was owned by the Graymen. Your peoples were being taxed for a war you never really understood. You never really understood why you had to fight; you never really understood why your children were conscripted to be slaughtered. You were never really told the untold story, you see. And then along came another President in a wisp of time, one who "had an accident." He didn't want to play ball because he did not want to install the Federal Reserve system of money control within your country. So he had a small, unfortunate accident. And so, guess what? You ended up with another President.

The Graymen really do tell you who's the best man for the office. They really want that person in office who is going to play ball for them. Throughout your naming of Presidents rather than kings, a lot of them have fallen by the wayside. And you're aware, a lot of them have been scandalized out of office. There has not been one President scandalized out of office by a scandal that was not perpetrated. Surprised? And all of your Presidents that have died were not killed by madmen, but rather because it was decided they were supposed to go. They weren't playing ball. Some of your Presidents found their conscience in the way. In other words, the God within them was waking up, saying, "This is not right. In all due consciousness, through the mercy of God, I cannot do this."

Well, Graymen have offices in various places. The subject of your President not playing ball would be brought up at a meeting, and they would simply say, "Get rid of him." The next person in line, of course, would be the person who would come in and continue on, status quo. Are your eyes open? Because you are seeing in print what only a few entities have ever dared to share with you! And I'm very daring, I suppose.

The families of the Graymen, by 1920, had grown to twelve families. They were the individuals who owned the international banks and, literally, Switzerland itself. They were the ones who had decided that gold would no longer be convenient to carry around. They were the ones who created paper money. They created the Bank of London; they *own* the Bank of London. They created a major Federal Reserve in every major country, in which *they* print paper money according to their desire and their plans for power.

Only the Shadow Knows

Finally in your country, after a few unfortunate incidents, the Federal Reserve Act was passed. That meant the Federal Reserve could now print monies in your country, *paper* money that was not necessarily backed by gold reserves. In other words, your paper money is worthless. The Graymen created an economy based on worthless pieces of paper because of their manipulative control. Not too many years ago it was against the law for Americans to own gold; it all had to be turned back in. Gold, you must understand, has been the bartering power for the last three thousand years. The more the Graymen could strip away the sense of value from any one human being, the more controllable that being became. Are you with me?

So now the Federal Reserve is incorporated. It prints "In God We Trust" on your paper money. It is run by an appointed director, who is appointed by an executive committee, whatever that is, that is appointed by the President; and the President is often appointed by — the shadows, yes.

The Federal Reserve is a banking system that *loans* your country money, yet it does not loan your country *enough* money to pay back the interest on what you borrow. So, if you are a little short, and your overseas goods aren't selling as well as they should be, you never, *ever* pay off the loan because it is incurring interest, since you only have the paper money that was issued to you. So you start doing strange and wonderful things, like mortgaging everything and selling different things, pieces of your country and the like. Your great melting pot, this model for freedom, is selling itself in order to facilitate a national debt! Don't you find it precarious that your country is in debt to itself? How odd; I always thought it was *very* precarious. Whom do you owe your debt to? To ensure that this debt would be paid off, the income tax was raised *just a little bit more*. And then, on Black Tuesday, everyone lost everything they had in the fall of the stock market. The value of their stocks plunged frantically, and people plunged out of windows in New York. That was quite wonderful to the Graymen; the controlling families who had people in important places were given the right legally to buy up *powerful, immense* wealth at bargain-basement prices. The crash was planned as well.

Now you owe a burdensome, unmerciful tax, paying against a dollar value which the Graymen control. Your Federal Reserve is not owned by any of you. It's not owned by your government — it is owned by itself.

Your country was falling rapidly into debt. The depression was upon you; nature wasn't cooperating, or so it was said. And people were going hungry, standing in bread lines — do you remember those days? You were trying to find a way to leap out of a sluggish economy and out of poverty. So, World War II was created.

The Financing of Megalomania

Do you think the monster Hitler would have been anyone had he not been financed? Don't you understand that the financiers who financed Germany at that time were playing on the megalomania of Hitler? In other words, they played on the lust in his altered ego for absolute power.

Let me tell you, that limited entity had such a craving for ultimate power that he envisioned himself as *world* emperor.

Hitler envisioned himself to be *the* number one person of the entire world, and he was given enough strokes by those who supported him to convince him he could do it. Hitler definitely had allegiance to his country, but he also needed a way to continue to confiscate wealth. He did so by destroying a very precious people, all in the name of legitimate robbery.

I want you to know something. A bank in New York helped finance Hitler. The banks of England financed him, though they were at war with him. Your natural resources — your nickel, your coal — all the raw products Germany did not possess as a natural resource were *shipped* to them. Where do you suppose they acquired the metal to create their war machines? From all the countries that were literally owned by the Graymen. Hitler was very well armed, do you recall?

Soon everyone said, "There is a terrible atrocity occurring in Germany. I suppose we should get into it." And the politicians were wailing, "We cannot let the greatness of America wane when her very allies are under attack by this monster . . . and if we do not do something quickly, we will not be able to suppress communism, Marxism, and yes, even the threat of Stalin. We must go to war to preserve liberty."

Listen: it was a game, unfortunately created. But blessed common people sent their children off to war, to die painfully alone in cold, blood-soaked and muddy trenches while the economy rose in this country, and people were making more money, and the standard of living rose and everyone was happy, except for those who were dying in the trenches, alone. This war was financed, of course, from your side of the water. And naturally, when more money was needed to place *your* war machinery into operation, your taxes were raised *just a little bit more* and your national debt was increased monstrously.

Did you learn that you won the war? Did anyone ever tell you that? Maybe you read about it, the *Victory!* Have you studied it in your history books? You *didn't* win the war. The Graypersons who instigated the war still live in their elite wealth and are still running this world. The true conquerors behind the horsemen escaped the skirmish without a scratch. And not *one* of their sons went to war. Their wealth has increased *enormously* from that action.

There's so much to tell you of this dance. What to tell you and what not to tell you . . . it is my dilemma to decide what is important for you to know at this point. Know this. There will never be a long march again, not in this dark age of the tyrants.

The Shadow Grows

THE BANKERS HAVE become international. They have loaned magnanimously. You thought you loaned to your country and caused it to incur its national debt? Do you think you're paying yourself back every time you pay your taxes? You're paying the Graymen *huge* profits. Yours is a nation that's too much in debt to loan anything to anyone. Yet, astoundingly, your bankers *continue* to loan to poor, struggling countries! Where do the bankers harvest the money to loan, if you are so bankrupt?

The bankers say they are lending in an attempt to lift these poor countries into the twentieth century; to lift them up economically. In most of these places, the people desire to have a democracy. They want to live like the Americans do, the Yanks; they've a real desire for that, so they are ripe for revolution.

So, in march the insurgents. Next they mix in a military government, and you have the necessary polarity. Then, of course, you have a need to develop the country, to support these people crying for democracy. The military government is only there temporarily. It is only there to feed, even further, the desire for freedom and liberty. Are you beginning to understand the process? The munitions dealers make lots of money. Munitions arrive from various Christian countries; they've been shipped from all over the world, even this country. Of course, this is all done in the name of business for the people that are *fighting* for democracy!

Once the change has begun, this poor farmer who once lived tranquilly upon his land, who didn't have to pay taxes, who could feed his family, who loved his God and his Church, is now

25

working in a fervor. Then he finds himself marching in strange streets of strange cities, asking for democracy, and he isn't quite sure *why* he is doing this. He's a part of social consciousness that has been intentionally created by the Graymen to support their image of world power. Of course, we all know that democracy wins out, and the big, bad communist military insurgents are whipped to the side, so liberty flies free again! And what does this young, tentative country need now? It needs substantial *loans* to develop a nation, to make it like the Yanks, indeed, like the Americans.

The minute the insurgents march out, the bankers march in, only too happy to give them *billions*. Do you know that term? More than a few scheckles — billions of that paper stuff; you know, it makes a nice fire. They loan the billions, knowing full well that those wonderful people who are there to lead this new *democratic* government will squander the money. The Graymen *know* it's going to be squandered; they know that little country won't be able to pay its loans.

So the banks have to call their notes. The leader responsible for the country pleads, "But we just don't have any money to make this loan payment." And the bank representative smiles, "Sir, that's quite all right. Eh, I'm sure we can work something out here. We will trade off your *substantial* debt for the natural mineral rights in your country, and all oil found off your shores and in your country. We'll take that in exchange." The leader responsible for the country is so happy, he says, "What a deal!"

So that's what they do. And now the little country isn't a *country* anymore. Certainly it's trying to make it as a democracy, but it's not really a country anymore. It's part of a borderless ownership that is growing steadily in your world today.

Can you guess how many Third World countries have had their loans called in recently? Quite a few. You'd be amazed at how quickly the Graymen get down to business and how settled the land becomes after that. Industry moves in; *things* outside of the control of the people take over because *they* have moved in; the proud natives of the land are swept off their land and herded into the cities. It doesn't matter if the farmers don't farm any longer. It doesn't matter if the rain forest is torn up into splinters. It just doesn't matter — developers are moving in, cutting down the forests, financed by the international bankers, all in the service of what you call progress.

And the natives are wondering: why are they hungry in the cities? And where is the other-worldly assistance that was scheduled to come in to sustain them, those economic adventures called export/import? Well, some of it arrives from the country of the Bear; they are told to ship it in. Do you know where the country of the Bear imported *their* goods from? From *you.*

At present there are only *three* countries in the *world* who are not absolutely owned by the Brotherhood of Graymen — *absolutely* owned. Two of these countries are at war, and one has sort of been forgotten, in a sense. Every other country, including Russia, is controlled by the Graymen.

Have you heard the term Bolshevik? Who do you think gave money to Lenin? How did Lenin materialize out of nowhere to implement his idealistic society? How was he able to overthrow the last Czar through a revolution, unmercifully murdering all of the Czar's family, ridding Russia of every aristocrat to incorporate his Marxist theory? The revolution was financed by the same bankers to create the *stigma* of communism, which would create many illusions in the future. Russia has the largest gold supply in the world — they do. They also were ripe for a new form of government, and they got it. The New World Order is taken from the writings of Marx, who was an elitist. He borrowed his idea from Socrates. And God knows where Socrates found his idea, but it was refined by every leader since then, who claimed it as "original" thinking.

Why is Marxism such an idealistic governing philosophy? Simply because it envisions a world controlled by an elitist few. Meaning that the people who are responsible, wealthy and powerful control the world and its people's "animalistic" attitudes. Marx said the common people have no intelligence. And the greatest danger to communism, and indeed to *this* theory of

Marxism, if you will, is that it cannot ever have what is called a mediocracy, a medium or middle class. The people *had* to be suppressed, controlled, their schooling governed, everything — that was the idealistic society. And that society has been instigated, created, and financed for many levels of purpose, the ultimate being what the final design of this society will be in a few years — the new World Order.

Communism had to be created. And in Russia, just like in the smaller countries, revolutions appeared out of nowhere. One minute the peasants were farmers; the next they were soldiers. First there has to be a polarity to induce the people to beg for new rulership, for change — there has to be a *threat*. If it weren't for the worldwide *threat* of communism, what would the munitions dealers have made these last few years? If it were not for communism, who would have been your enemy? Cuba? Do you understand? Listen, because of *created* communism, the American people have always feared a threat to their liberty. Because of that communistic society, the American people have gotten their nose into everyone else's business, because they were told to, because *communism* is a threat to liberty. All along it has been a manipulation, indeed a game.

Do you think the people of the Bear are ruthless and hard? Do you think they are without a soul? Do you think that within them lies no wonderment of what created all of this? Do you think that when they work with the simple earth they don't wonder at the seasons, and at the growth of a singular seed into food upon the plate? They are just like *you,* for they are children, Gods of the Living Force. Why have they been afraid of you? Because *their* media is owned and their people are told precisely what you imperialistic capitalists are like!

Don't you think that, had it been up to them *directly,* they would have opened their borders to you? And you to them? An exchange of brotherhood and life, rather than an unnatural line of demarcation. Imagine the control, imagine the control of one man who can control an entire nation of human beings. It demands a great altered ego.

Your brothers that you label communists? They are *your* brothers, they are your sisters; they do not hate you. They do not understand you any more than you do them, and the barriers have been intentionally kept that way. Don't you find a wall made out of iron the most hideous slap in the face to humanity you have ever seen? I was there one day in your time and looked upon it. A wall that can keep *out* a whole nation of people? Amazing!

This may seem tedious to you. It may seem irrelevant to your important life, to the decisions you make, to the way you live. What bearing could this have on you? Don't you understand that this is the same attitude that has allowed this tyranny to flourish in the world? At present, your country, though you call it America, does not exist. Your Constitution, the reflective piece of paper of the vision of democracy, your rights that are Bills that you can enact, is the only thing that holds the fabric of your liberty together. But there has been so much manipulation and bylaws and interpretations, so much programming.

And most importantly, your country has grown fat and lazy on its cans. How did this happen? Through subtle social indoctrination. When your physical embodiments were generated from your forefathers and your foremothers, they were seeded with the emotional fervor of freedom. They were not warlords; they wanted away from battle. You have a natural inclination not to make war, except on your neighbor.

Why did you want your freedom? To live in joy, the *pursuit of happiness,* remember? You wanted to toil in the fields, labor in the cities, drink your brew, collect your wages fairly earned, go out and party hearty . . . and have lunch. Lunch?! Why don't you just say, "Let's go eat!" *Lunch.* So here you are — you lunch, you are entertained after work and on weekends, and when you are home you sit back and watch a box; why, it's on all the time! Your whole world is centered around this box — it entertains you, it hypnotizes you, it controls your emotions, and your whole life is *lived* by the dramas you witness. What do you care who runs the country as long as you have your wages, your brew, your entertainment, and your days off — *paid.*

Don't you know that couched in that peaceful lethargy is the remarkable attitude that is the reason why this country, indeed the *world,* is ruled by tyrants? Because the people don't want to be bothered. They don't want to hear *bad* news. They don't want to have to go out and vote — what a nasty thing! It was raining. The system doesn't work anyway. They don't want to be bothered by the decision-making process in this country. They would rather play games on shows than hear the news. Painful, aye? In other words, libertarians have, for the most part, been creatures of the past.

Every person who has stood up and spoken out, who has endeavored to enlighten, to gain an awareness for the sleeping, dreaming middle class, has been ridiculed into non-existence. The irony is, they were not simply ridiculed out of the picture by the Graymedia, but by the people they were attempting to awaken. Listen: the sleeping people of America are doing the work of the Graymen's dream. The *people* are fulfilling the Graymen's image of their world order! All the television or the newspaper has to do is to tell you that someone is insane, or that there was some indiscretion in his or her past. That's all the sleeping masses need to laugh that person off the podium. The people are doing it *for* the Graymen.

Politicians Aren't Born . . .

Now, let's take a look at your country and your last King. Your past King, — President, as you call him (it's just a different title, he just doesn't wear a crown) — he was everything that the American people wanted. He *was;* thus, he was considered weak by the Graymen. He was considered a libertarian. He was also considered to be a famous person, and Americans idolize famous people. He was idealistic and put where he is. (By the way, you will never see a Grayman's face in the papers or on the box. You won't hear anything about them; they remain anonymous. They choose that. It's best for business.)

I want you to know something about your last King. He *is* a great man. And there is also another reason why this entity was where he was. He has not completely been the anonymous puppet you may imagine. Your last President also has within him a great love for God and righteousness. The Graymen think that anyone who believes in God is a superstitious idiot; and they also realize that they can utilize that superstition, and their *disbelief,* to work to their advantage. And they have.

This last President, I want you to know, loves God as he knows it. He has a great conscience, for your information. While he was in office, he prayed every single night for guidance. I know; I've listened. His desire to upgrade your war machine was righteous, for like the middle-class people, he also saw that liberty could be threatened at any time by the communists. He was very naive. He saw that it was important to rebuild the strength of this great nation, so that it would forever have the power to protect its borders, its allies, and its image. The people loved him.

He immediately went to work to reestablish your centurion guards at your door. It took a lot of gold to do that and the Federal Reserve was only too willing to lend it — they loved him too. The munitions makers loved him, because he was increasing armaments in this country. And he thought he was doing the right thing; you must understand that.

As his term waned and he became more aware of what was around him, and what was *truly* at work in the world, the man desperately endeavored to try to change it. Still within his soul lies an innocence and a libertarian that is indeed kind and loves this, his country. Feebly he worked, very diligently, on endeavoring to keep foreign investment out of your country. He could see that foreign investors were intentionally buying up barren farmland, intentionally buying up real estate, intentionally buying up corporations. He was making moves to keep that from happening because your country belonged to the people; not to other people, but to *its* people.

And it was on a rainy morning that the full realization of what exactly had been ruling the world came to him. For the first time, he saw why he could not make the decisions he wanted to make, and he became severely ill. He trusted no one. Did you hear that he wouldn't talk to anyone? He couldn't. He had no one to converse with about what he was feeling. Your King struggled to bring to the surface, through the media, the concept of creating the American Central Bank that would be the bank of the American people. He thus endeavored, in his own way, to create America's own money. It was never as fully investigated as many of his other affairs were. And the man that was to help him in this little matter was removed from his post. The name of this man was Volker.

This, your last President, was one of three that will, in the final analysis, bring about Solon's Republic, Superconsciousness.

By the way, I don't vote. I do not campaign; this is not politics. It was a great writer, Cicero, who said, "Politicians aren't born, they are excreted!" Yes.

But this man, your past President, endeavored to hold himself together with all this weight bearing upon his consciousness. Even at the very end of his term, he was in the last throes of trying to do the right thing and he just didn't know how to go about it.

Listen, he *desired* for your *In God We Trust* dollar, you know, your paper money, to fall. He was hoping that if it fell, you Americans wouldn't look like such a lucrative business investment to outside investors. There was a meeting of the Graymen and great bankers in the year called eighty-seven in your time. In the latter part of January and again in February, there was a meeting; heads of all families were represented, and there was the most powerful representation of the East. At this meeting they became more aware of your King's desire, and they decided to threaten calling their loan.

The American people cannot *possibly* pay back to the Graymen the debt that is now incurred, the debt that you owe to *their* Federal Reserve. They continue to use the strategy of pushing up your economy through the naiveté of your Presidents. And when Reagan understood what was occurring, they simply stated this: "Unless you support the taxation of your people to render this debt, the moneymakers who have invested heavily in your market will pull out." They are calling their loans. No more money will come into your country.

What does that all mean? Well, you received a little taste of it not too long ago. Playing the gambling game — you know, the bottom dropped out of the Market, as it's called. And that little slap in the face was only to show you they can flex their muscles. What would it mean if that little country called Japan, whose people are rallying from their miserable debts, were to pull out all of their money from your Market? It only takes *one* man who owns the majority of stock at the present time to create an absolute crash. And such a man is one of the people who's threatening.

This also works in harmony with another one of the Graymen's plans, that America no longer really be a sovereign country, but, instead, become dependent on outside trade. Therefore, America cannot close the door on outside trade, even though you are buying up more of someone else's product then you are your own. And no one really wants to buy your products; they're too busy building up their *own* economy. A deal has been made to your disadvantage. Its result is that you cannot put regulations on anyone, nor on the amount of products sent to your country.

So, no more closed-door policy. And then came a law that you had to buy these traded goods, because, you see, the Graymen own the other countries. And they have said, "You will pay back this loan. You are going to tax your people. You are going to cut their wages. You will put a freeze on purchasing and your people will have to pay for this. Because if you don't, this is what we will do." And your last President was reticent regarding raising your taxes any more than they have already been raised.

Your President wasn't budging, even though he began to be publicly ridiculed. What is it you called him toward the end of his term? A lame donkey? Donkey, or *duck,* whatever. Please! You say a lot worse words than that. What does *lame duck* mean? You were openly making a fool of him! And the men that are Gray know precisely what they're doing. Because now, the peoples who are representative of the One World Order are in a very specific party movement. And they went further to insult that last

King, making him look old, decrepit, and incapable of thinking properly. Quite the contrary! They wanted you to think this, because they are moving in for the kill.

To prove a point to you I'll add this. You don't want your taxes raised, so the American people say, "No, no, *no*," and they change channels . . . on a television, of course. (Small jest, yes, a celestial jest.) Your last President, Reagan, was holding out; he would not raise your taxes. Toward the end he opened himself only to his wife's confidence, for he trusted no one, he felt he could talk to no one, and he prayed relentlessly for guidance. And now you have a new King!

Tree Shakers

The Graymen wanted to shake a few trees to show some people just how powerful they are. To wake up this wonderful, lethargic society you live in, those who truly control the stock market did a little number on you. It was just a warning, but they wanted it to be so catastrophic that the whole public's attention would be centered on your National Debt. They wanted you to think your National Debt was the reason that the bottom dropped out of the Market. That is not the reason that it went down! It was *supposed* to go down. It was manipulated as another game, and what do *they* care how much *you* lost? They are the ones that print the money. They do not care! If your life savings were there, do you think they would be concerned? No, they would not. They are elitist. If they want more money, they *print* it.

They created Black Monday's five-hundred-point loss to stress something to you. What was being said that week? "Everyone had better wake up and do something about our debt, because America is bankrupt; they're calling their loans, pulling their money out of the Market. Why, our economy is so shaky," *gasp,* "even foreign investors are backing off."

All the investors playing the Market were staring down at your King, screaming, "You gotta do something about this! I'm losing everything!!" *What a wonderful way for the Graymen to get implemented what they want!*

The bottom line is, in order to protect your investments, you are willing to take on more taxes in order to pay back the loan that will never be paid back.

At that point, your King had no one to talk to. Not only did he feel the pressure of those who were around him, but he had realized the true power in the world. And he walked around his White House those last months muttering, "God help us. God help us." And he felt the pressure of the media because everyone will see this ". . . *awful horror.* The whole world's economy is shaky because of America's greedy spending," because of *your* indebtedness. And you are playing right into their hands.

Do you think there are very many countries that are very happy with you and their economic state at the present time? What do you think they think of you? What they are told to think of you.

And sure enough, your President says, "I will talk about this. Indeed, we will consider raising the taxes." He does not want to, but they are pressing him hard. And in the end, my beloved friends, you are going to have *unmerciful* taxes placed upon you. Your standard of living will not rise anymore. The income-producing status of your labor will not be able to increase any longer. In other words, you will work as hard or *harder,* and you will not make any more money. And all you wondrous elderly people, who have been putting money in your government — rather, I should say, they are taking it from you — to insure that you will have a place to live in your *twilight* years, well, you're not going to see that money because that security system is bankrupt as well.

And the farmers in your country will continue to be forced into bankruptcy, as is happening every day. The middle class that supports the elite and the rabble in the streets will now take on a further burdensome tax, to take care of everyone. *Everyone.* It is part of their attempt to break the potential power momentum in your country. The harder you have to work and the less your buying power, the more docile you become, the more you become part of their One World Order.

The man involved in Watergate? What was his name? Who was the King? Nixon? Toward the end of his reign he endeavored to do the same as your last King. He knew all about your gold situation. He knew all about the oil prices that were fixed. He knew all about everything that was under siege, and he tried to bring it to public notice in the end. What was the result of his turning on those who had supported him? They set him up; for what crime did he, in truth, commit?

I haven't painted a very pretty picture for you. I would be much happier chatting with you about other celestial stuff, about the God within you, and all of those wonderful things that are at the apex of the human experience. You are not living in the Age of Enlightenment. You are living in the Age of Tyrants, and have been for some time now. The Graymen *own* the world. They do not see the world as individual democracies and they do not see it as made up of individual countries. They see no borders. Laws don't matter to them because they influence the law. They *own* the world because they have control of the money that runs the world.

America isn't really the *Home of the Free* as it had been created to be. Once it was.

But you have been asleep, prattling, talking idly at great length, babbling. You have not stood up with the backbone and fervor of libertarians to say, "*Enough!*" For what are thirteen families and international bankers against a whole nation of pissed-off people? I borrowed the term because I understand what it means to you — severely angry, yes!

Their Lust for Power
Is Endless

W HAT IS LIFE? How could it be lived? Outside of your train-
ing and your indoctrination, what could it mean to live
life?

Most of you could not even conceive of living without money.
Most of you think of sovereignty only to the limits of your
freedom of choice. You think that certain things, such as bearing
up under the yoke of unmerciful taxation, increasing your indebtedness, earning lower wages, seem to be normal in life. You
accept them and so they are exempt from the word sovereignty.

Sovereignty is absolute liberty from any and all things that own
you. There *are* sovereign people in your country. They have
created a life from the land that nurtures them, yet they are free
people. Of course, they do not live in style, as you would term it.
They do not own auto machines, necessarily. They do not have
cloths of silver and gold. They do not have silk and Persian
carpets upon their floors, and they do not eat out of silver dishes.
But they're *free,* and they've been that way for quite a while.
Because they incur no income, and they live on what their land
produces and what they can barter and trade.

But for the most part, Americans cannot live without your
burgers. You cannot conceive of *not* doing business with your
bank. You cannot conceive of purchasing without the card because it's *chic* and you are an "*in*" person. And you cannot
conceive of living without all of your things.

37

If only your last King could have had the courage to hold out, against all odds. You have to understand, the people in America do not know what is going on; they only know what the tele tells them. If your King could have held out, the Graymen would have declared *war* on America and your stock market would have been ruined *the very next day,* at the opening bell, because they control its flux. They would have pulled out all of their money in this government and would have called their loan. For what good is the loan? It is only paper. The people of this country would have been put into the severest depression they have ever known, certainly the most severe that most of you would have ever known.

And yet, ultimately, it would have been the grandest opportunity to be free from tyrants that control and rule your very lives. For how *will* you stop their rule of the lives of your children, and your children's children? When will freedom declare itself? Yet, no one understands that simple twist, nor can they see the future sunrise of it, because most of you have never made it your business to investigate why.

But as it is seen in this hour, you *will* be taxed. And your incomes will be frozen or lessened. And you will be put *painfully* to the yoke to pay for something that will *never* be paid for. That is how it is in this hour.

Don't They Have Enough?

What is the aim of these Gray people? What is it they *want?* Is it not enough that they own all the money in the world? Isn't that enough? Is it not enough that they control the companies that own all the oil in the world? Do you think the Arabs own their oil? No, they were naive nomads who took loans to develop their fields. How else could they build their refineries? They don't own their oil; they own hot, blowing sand.

Don't the Graymen have enough? What more could they want? They're destroying the rain forest. Do you know why the rain forest is being destroyed in the Southern Hemisphere? Do you care? The destruction of the rain forest is being perpetuated by real estate investors, by bankers and developers. Do you think they care that they are destroying the atmosphere that holds up your sky? They don't care. It's for greed that leads to power. What are you going to breathe?

What is it the Graymen want? They desire *absolute* power, the absolute power to create their ideal of One World Order. It's changing names now, but what does *One World Order* truly mean? That the whole world would be one nation of invisible borders. It would be governed by a sort of social fascism. The elite will rule you all; you will be enslaved. The selling point behind this One World Order is that there will be no more wars; and with one world government, you will be told everyone is equal. Except the elite. And the elite will allow humanity to progress without revolution, without war, without pestilence, to further their aristocracy.

In other words, middle-class America and the free people who live in far-off places that you don't even know of are indeed to become slaves. And many of you deserve it because you've created the vacuum in which it can occur. You want to be told what to do; you want someone to make decisions for you; you don't want to be bothered with it. You want someone to tell you what's going to happen next year because you don't want to be bothered. That is a One World Order.

Now, we are getting to the crux of it all. This One World Order can only come into play if there is *one* World Bank. And if there is one World Bank, why bother with rupees and yens, and marks and dollars? This is the reasoning they will use on you. "Why do we have to worry about the flux of the economy? Look at the trauma it causes in the stock market, in the world money markets! Well, we had to worry up until this point, but we won't need to any longer." Rather than printing *worthless,* widely fluctuating paper, they will issue a universal card called the *Debit Card.* You've heard of it? You can take this little card and go anywhere in the world, punch in anyplace you want to punch in, and everyone will take it, gladly.

Now, there's a slight problem with this card — just a tiny, little problem of privacy and freedom. Everything will be known about *everyone* who takes this card. Everything you purchase will be known, everywhere you go will be known. Everything you *do* will be known! The freedom of privacy will no longer exist, because without this card, you will not be able to purchase or *sell* anything. The common exchange that you are familiar with, decimal dollars and cents, will be done away with. And everyone will have a number. And it will be your number until the end of your life. And everyone who has this number will have a file. And anyone who gets out of line will simply be rendered neutral.

What if you go to the market and you lay down your dollars and cents for bread, and the clerk says to you, "We do not accept dollars and cents any longer; we only take your card"? And you walk to the next baker and he tells you the same thing. And you spend your whole day searching for a loaf of bread that no one will sell to you because your dollar is worth nothing to them. You return home without bread, for you have no garden and no food, for you are cosmopolitan *hungry* Americans. And the only way you will get the bread is to have the card.

And with your card, your taxation will be taken care of, automatically. With your card, your bank accounts will be taken care of, automatically. With your card, you will *never* see any energy exchange for your labor, because your labor exchange will be electronically transmitted from your employer to your bank. And every item that you purchase will be automatically debited from your energy exchange. It's already happening.

This magical card was proposed to the people of Australia, and it so outraged them that they voted it down. It was most daring of the Graymen to put the card up publicly for a vote. And it was handily defeated; that was the reaction of the people *down under,* because even the simplest person understood the implications of The Card.

The sell in your country is very subtle. They're not going to tell you unless you ask your banker, "Do I have a debit card, a debit file?" The selling of the card is being approached in America through great commercials. Commercials — a crier in the market-place. Everything is being automated and programmed to be put on the card. You can even purchase a home now on a card — just charge a home; yes, that is the truth! Charge this, charge that. Everything is charged.

It's a way to slowly move your awareness to the card — the *ultimate* card. They're selling you the way they've always sold you, whether they want you to vote for a politician, whether you should take action in this war, pass this bill, or buy soap suds. They've always sold you. The sale of the card is already happening — the ultimate card will take care of everything!

Are you in for a shock? The majority of the people who will read this book, who do business with a bank, already *have* their number. That's right; those of you who live off this seductive plastic card will soon be switched over, subtly, to your own debit card. The propaganda has already started.

But there is another intrigue that awaits in the wings. Before the debit card can truly be implemented, your stock market must be destroyed. Your stock market affects *all* markets that will be replaced by the economic governing board of the new World Order. Consequently, it must be collapsed. When it collapses, all markets will be sucked into the vacuum created, into the tentacles of the debit-card authority.

It is already falling in ruins, because what occurred not too long ago was a lesson aimed at your government. The lesson? To wake up the people so they will start pointing a finger, because people can become very kind until it comes to the issue of money. And then they can become very hostile. Hauntingly enough, the One World Order is already in place at various levels throughout various countries in your world.

The altered ego of man, the altered *you,* is the image that I refer to as an Antichrist. And truly, this current push towards *ultimate* control does not emanate from the divineness within the human being, that righteousness and glory that is within the great ego.

It is coming from an image the Grayman souls have lived up to, lifetime after lifetime. It is the repetition, over and over again, of always suppressing that divine aspect that allows the evolution of the human spirit, the manifested destiny of God, to occur.

Wickedness — there are those who do believe in devils and Satan and all of that, but there are no such entities. Wickedness is a choice, a mere process of good or bad in the form of an altered ego, an altered *you*. Wickedness is a natural emotional state within an altered ego. When I speak of *wickedness,* I am not talking about crimes against the state. I am talking about crimes that are against self and self's reflection upon its neighbor.

The altered ego *chooses* tyranny and also chooses its own victimization. Wickedness lies, *by choice,* in the image of man and woman, for by choice we can love rather than hate. By *choice* we can be tolerant rather than intolerant. By *choice* we can engender the gentility of the spirit rather than the unmercifulness of the spirit. By *choice* we can *allow* rather than make war. And by *choice* we choose, inevitably, what we will live in manifested destiny.

Wickedness is a *choice* of the individual. To suppress another under the guise and aims of your own image is a tyranny, whether it is through the suppression of your neighbor, your lover, your husband, your wife, or your children. If the act of suppression is committed in the image of the altered ego, it is wickedness. And when it is perpetrated on a worldwide scale, it is indeed also wicked, by choice.

The altered ego of a man is much different from his soul/spirit reflection within. They are almost in complete juxtaposition. Conscience, the *feeling* of righteousness — indeed love, allowance, nurturing, compassion, the love of the All that is the intricacy of life — is all within the soul. But these feelings of total fulfillment and splendid grandeur are suppressed for the glory of the altered ego, indeed the Antichrist. There is not *one* Grayman that is not endowed with God within him. He is not wicked in his soul. Their handmaidens, they are not wicked in their souls. They are, by choice, facilitating their image and the lust for power that is the apex of the altered ego. It is endless, yet changeable in an instant.

It is not enough that they own the world's gold. It is not *enough* that they own all the fossil fuels under the earth. It is not enough that they destroyed the rain forest for development. It is not enough that they pit one brother against another brother for the purpose of greed. That is power. But the ultimate ejaculation of ecstasy for the image is to own the world and be "The Sovereign."

These Gray People are driven through heritage, through their aims and their goals, to what they *must* fulfill. Their goal is no different from yours. Yours is for sovereignty; theirs is for absolute power — the same energy. They *have* to fulfill it. It is their destiny — *destiny*. The ultimate destiny of the altered ego is power. And greed — *greed* — is the way they acquire it. A poor man can buy respect in the twinkling of an eye when he becomes an heir. And a rich man fears losing everything by becoming poor.

The Gray Ones are forced, by altered ego, into their trauma. Even within their families they hate one another. Why? Because one of them is *Number One* — Ishna, my term — and they all want to be. They all want to be Number One, so they hate one another and they have violent wars between one another. And often thousands of people die over a simple dispute. They do not care.

And the Beast Fed on a Number

These entities are approaching their ultimate victory march in manifested destiny, for they have succeeded in their long-range plan, up until this hour. And if anyone stood in their way, they did away with them. They got them out of the picture. The Graymen are aligned, and they are obsessed with their goals.

There is only one thing in manifested destiny that will eradicate this, and that is knowledge. Knowledge: you *waking up*! There is a prophecy in your Book of books, the one Book that wasn't tampered with. *Revelations* — an appropriate term. The author prophesied hideous things in the last days. Well, if you were John of old, and an angel manifested a vision of a computer, a very *big* computer, blinking at you, humming, wheeling, turning, churning, ominous, and you'd never seen one of these before, wouldn't you rather refer to it as a beast? Of course you would.

John saw, through a vision of actual manifested destiny, the climactic moments of the very times you are living in. And the beast fed on a number, and the number was 666. Heard you of that? Yes, it's become sort of an avoided thing to have added onto any part of your person. But 666 is six, meaning the number of man. And 666 means a tally of gold. And the embossment of the mark of the beast is represented such that the beast is embossing the six, which is the number of man, and 666, through a tally of gold.

Those who take this Debit Card will be *owned*. They will have given up their liberty and their freedom. They will have fortified themselves with the beast and, indeed, the atheistic destiny of their controllers. You give up absolute choice and freedom when the vacuum becomes so severe that the vacuum collapses. The law of that collapse is change, and those who take The Card will be changed.

John's prophecy is a rightfully truthful prophecy. And it is on its way, rolling out in destiny, coming to pass. Why is it warned that you should not take The Card? It goes back to choice. Remember *choice:* you *can* make the decision; you are *free* to make the decision. You can come and go wherever you choose. You can choose to believe or not to believe this communiqué. You can choose everything in your reality, which the lot of you have done since the beginning of this existence. You even chose how you were to come back genetically — yes, you did; you selected this space/time for its promises of adventure, and you won't be disappointed.

The End of Time

What happens to the inalienable Law of God when the vacuum of choice and life no longer exist? And what happens to the glorified human being when, innately, its divine right of choice is collapsed? That which is on the horizon will deny you the right of absolute choice in freedom. And what you have created is an ending of time, an ending of the time-flow. An end to the process of life rolling forward. An end to the creation within your reality of everything necessary for the immortal soul to evolve towards that immaculate human being. An end of the opportunity to live unto the Light of Christ.

But this is still a matter of choice. It takes guts to change. It takes *guts* to go forward into the unknown for the adventure. But it is only in the unknown that one embraces evolution, indeed change.

You cannot evolve in your adventure without changing; and change is by choice, indeed *option.* Change is *natural,* yes, nature — the All within the All. But when the option to change no longer exists — when you can no longer evolve because of spurious control — then life as you know it, that was the glory of God as you have expressed it, comes to an end.

And end it would. For what is the use of the God manifest in human flesh if it neither toils nor spins the wheel? And what indeed is the use of an anvil? A plow? What is the use of land and harvest when there is no freedom to enjoy it? And what is the use of the laughter of children if they will soon be put to the yoke?

There *is* no purpose, no reason for life. What could the purpose be, if freedom of choice were collapsed?

It will be in that moment when you will hear a great voice echoed from the furthermost star, a voice that emanates through all things that are alive and living. And the voice will say, "It is finished!"

Thus will begin Superconsciousness.

You Are Living in the Greatest Times of the Human Drama

Choice is very precious in these days of yours. Oh, I know, you will put this book down and go back to perceiving everything as secure. There is food on the shelf. You are warm and toasty in your home. You don't have to get your hands dirty. Your lover calls, or you call, or however all that goes about. Things seem to be more real, unthreatened. You look outside and everything's peaceful, tranquil; the birds are singing, animals are going to and fro. How could any of this truth fit into some natural order? Well, because you see what you want to see. You hear what you want to hear. You've allowed what you want to allow. But you are living in the greatest times of the human drama. The very end of this adventure, where choice, and the inalienable right to have it through the creator that gave unto you the light of what you are, comes to an end.

You know, the war of darkness and light has long been prophesied. It happens on many levels. You ought to remember that darkness and light having a battle would be a most peculiar thing to see, because you would think that the light would penetrate the darkness or vice versa. But what I am speaking of is an unseen freedom coming to the point where it has to make a decision to be that way, in what seemingly is the normal world.

And just like you have a choice about whether to read this or not, you are also going to make choices in the times to come that are going to be pertinent for you for the rest of your life. And what is really worth anything if you can no longer live the glory of God within you in absolute, brilliant light? And what is freedom really all about? What is having liberty all about? It is the right to choose. It is the right to live, which has been so wonderfully demonstrated. When you don't have those any longer, you have lost it all.

The altered ego of the Graymen has created the most wise individuals, perhaps, that you would ever know, because they know human nature. They know how you slave to your wants. And they know what you want to hear and what you *don't* want to hear. They know how to stroke you and how to threaten you. They understand the altered ego, because that is supremely what they act through. They know how to play on your patriotism, your liberty, your abundance.

Baiting the Trap

Your economy is in radical change at this moment. As it is seen now, your market that is so important to this country will face what seems like absolute destruction at a point in the not-too-distant future. But it'll get up again and struggle for three more years without really making any headway. This will put the people in a screaming mode, asking for reform. And it will come. The changes that will occur from this are going to be dramatic.

I want you to know something. You inherited a lot of this. You came into this plane, this country, this body, inheriting oftentimes the ignorance of your parents, inheriting acceptance of the rule of thumb. Most people think the Federal Reserve is owned by the federal government. It is not. Every major country has its own federal reserve. And that, my beloved entities, is what pulls the purse strings. Not a country, but a family.

The Trap

Economically you are in for some hard times, because in order for you to want what is the next step, you have to go through the pain and the sorrow that are coming. Most will go through it, because they feel that it is their duty to resolve this.

There has always been a trap. I don't care to what extent anyone argues best interests, or to what extent anyone argues that without wars and pestilence and greed there would not be any developing technology — *yes,* there would have been. And you would not have people closing up their farms that for generations have fed them and many others. You do now; wastelands are appearing. And without this greed, you would not have an atmosphere above your Earth that is growing more poisonous by the moment, with holes developing at many places in it, which you are going to read about. Holes in your atmosphere!

The Natural Price of Greed

What does this mean to you, right now, in the moment of reading this? It means a lot. For without this perpetrated greed, you would not have had massive destruction. Without this greed, your animal life would not be dying, nor would your great forests. And without the greed you would not have had the suppression of genius and you would have had more ingenious displays of the longevity of things that do not burn fossil fuels. Because of greed, you cannot afford to have new and more efficient ways of creating energy out front. Great ideas are stagnated, because of greed!

You are emptying poisons into the sea — the sea, of all places. And it has gone on for so long that your fish are dying in droves. They are throwing themselves upon your beaches, crying, "Where else can I go, for I am breathing and eating your excrement, your poison! Where else can I go to have you see what you're doing, but here on the land?"

Without this greed you would not have primeval forests dying. Without this greed you would have normal weather. Nature would be in continuous movement without erratic eruptions. And you could continue.

Everyone's got to make a living, you say? Yes, that is a truth. But not everyone was keen enough on the laws that allowed them to make a living. And though your future is now in manifested destiny, destiny is brought about by embracing an attitude and allowing the space for its acceptance.

This is where your world is. And that is what has occurred and is still occurring. It is not wrong or right. It is simply manifested destiny. Every moment you start your engines and put your pedal to the metal, you are widening the holes in the stratosphere. You are outraged about that, but what can you do? You still have to go to and fro? But you are outraged! What are you going to do?

You are really in a pickle — yes, you are. Because that is the accepted and expected virtue of cosmopolitan man and woman. And every time you buy a burger, you are supporting the necessity for the destruction of forests around the world so cattle can graze to satisfy the craving for burgers. And every time you throw away its container, all of the gases from that container are still going into the stratosphere. But they are disposable, so what the heck?

There are changes in the offing, having to do with the days to come, that are pertinent and meaningful for you, and for nature.

I will tell you something. It would be to your greater benefit to start rooting for nature. Because your greatest chance of a reprieve lies in the Earth's forward movement as it endeavors to heal the many wounds on its body, and in the process to destroy computers and the world banking systems. Because a zipper doesn't care what is sitting on it.

Where would you be without nature? Without Mother Earth? Where would you stand? Where would you build your house? Where would you pass excrement? Where would you be without this organism that is your Earth?

Because of the desire for power, lived vividly through greed, mankind and womankind have benefited in major ways through the advancement of technology. That is a truth. And yet, because of the need of greed and the advancement of what is coming, your Earth sort of looks like your body. Now, imagine your body covered with leprosy — open, bleeding sores. And what if you had major cuts on your body? Wouldn't you try to anoint them, heal them? And the wounds? Would you not try to clean them out? And what about the air that you were breathing? What if it was continuously noxious and caused you to be sick to your stomach? And the water that you drink? What if the water was filled with poison and bacteria and was eating away the interior of your physical body? And what if the clouds that were coming over your body every day were raining acid on top of you? Would you do something about it?

Well, the Earth is no different from your body, and you can't live without it. And I have given you just a few examples of the hurt this living organism has endured, and why it needs to do something in the face of greed and power to heal itself, lest it end up more liken unto its sister, the red planet, which once had a thriving civilization called humanity.

The Hope of Enlightenment

Now listen, you. I do not desire that you become disheartened, or that you become a fanatic either. I do not desire for you to think that where there is knowledge there is not hope, for there is. I do not wish you to think nor desire you to know that this whole mess is hopeless. It isn't. It smells, but it is not hopeless.

For understand this: enlightenment means to come out of ignorance and out of the darkness. When one stays in the darkness of ignorance, he is prone to superstitions and helplessness. He becomes very fearful. Enlightenment is to shed light on ignorance, to dispel superstition; indeed, to dispel fear. Knowingness is not something to be afraid of, but rather to draw to yourself so that it broadens your perception of your own reality, of your own life; inevitably, that affects the whole of humanity.

Feeding the Altered Ego

Social consciousness — the very manner, breath, and understanding that feeds the altered ego — is like your breath. Social consciousness is a thought process of recyclable thoughts. In other words, it's sort of like history repeating itself, over and over again. Not only on a broad scale when talking about an entire country, or an entire humanity, but also it is the same with individual life, individual reality. Social consciousness collectively is what keeps the altered ego, the Antichrist, the image functioning. It's the very foodstuff that feeds it.

Truth is everywhere. Social consciousness is truth. But in order to allow the absorbing of an altered ego, and on a mass scale to allow social consciousness to be dispelled, you must begin to broaden your own reality. You are in the process of evolution — you are evolving. You are evolving to your manifested destiny; the more you become aware, the greater your reality, the more control, options and choices that you have.

When Light Is Born

In social consciousness you are very limited. You have to do what everyone else does. And social consciousness stays intact because that's how everyone is. But when light is born into the world, when a reality is broadened, a perception is broadened. When enlightenment occurs, even to one singular individual, that individual, who has been a participant in the continuum of social consciousness, suddenly becomes aware of more truth, more understanding. The consciousness of that individual lifts social consciousness. For what is beginning to be perceived by one goes out, and begins to influence others.

The end result of human destiny will not be a descent into historic repetition. It is rather the destiny of the human being to evolve into a complete spiritual entity, to become an immaculate human being. That is your destiny — to manifest the righteousness and the virtues of Christ latent within each of you. That is the apex of this evolution. In God you are, for you have the right of choice.

Enlightenment is lifting and broadening your own consciousness through knowledge. It is not spiritual rituals. It *is* understanding.

In this book, to the dismay of some, I have chosen to bring forth a teaching of historical value. I have given you a clear understanding of the "why," coupled with an understanding of choice, coupled with an understanding of the image of the altered ego. I chose to bring this understanding forward so that you can no longer say no one ever gave you the answer to "why," to encourage you to come out of your ignorance.

I chose to enlighten you regarding your history to help you

ascertain a broader picture of what collective manifested destiny in the human being is all about and to give you the "why." So that you know, so that you have an understanding and are no longer a toy to superstition. So that you are no longer a toy to someone else's explanation of the way things are when they aren't that way at all. Certainly it was not to depress you. It was to broaden your understanding so that you can look out your window and see the lay of the land, and make choices to illuminate your path through it all.

Enlightenment for the master, for the spectacular human being, is as necessary as breathing. It is as necessary as sleeping, waking, doing. For without knowledge, you only remain a faceless humanity, lacking in individuality, merely echoing what others around you echo so that it can be passed on.

All that is written here is intended to give you an understanding of the days that are upon you. And in the unknown that lies outside your window, you will also learn of hope, of options and probabilities that exist in the unknown, doors that are only unlocked to those who broaden their perception through enlightenment to gain the answers. The unknown never comes to a closed-minded entity. It rarely comes to one who is swathed in fear, but rather to one who goes forward with the desire to understand.

So for those of you who have begun to feel powerless and hopeless in reading this, I desire you to know there really is no such thing as hopelessness. There is another side to this story that is yet untold, that is yet to be realized. And we will reach that point in the coming passages. So hold onto your hats and your brains, and your emotional souls, and learn. Learn — and never be afraid to learn. It is what will deliver you from this smelly mess. Bargain? So be it.

Nature – The Imbalance

Now, REMEMBER WHEN I told you to remember the name Rothschild? And remember when your marketplace of paper ran amuck and many, many entities lost much of their security in it? Well, I want to show you how powerful the Graymen are. This is just a small example. Know you fossil fuels? Petrol, Tyrannosaurus Rex liquified. Well, there was a great company in London that did their business in petrol. They decided to issue public stocks. Strange words, but those are the words that are appropriate. They decided to let the public buy into petrol.

It was wonderfully planned, because it was put out and made available to the public at large that they could be participants, holders, in fossil fuels. And then came the *dark day* in the financial world. And as a result, the public got frightened off. No one wanted to buy the offering. They had no money, couldn't hedge, bet, and all of that stuff. So, to step in and to pick up the slack, the Rothschilds bought it up! They are very wise individuals, for that allowed them to own more of a controlling mass of the fossil fuels. So it was very well planned.

Now, I want you to remember something. These people do not claim an allegiance to any of their heritage. And, again, to no country and to no religion. They are, in all senses of the words as you would term them, atheists. And their God is money, and their kingdom power. That's it — nothing else matters. So; here we have even more Graymen power put into Tyrannosaurus Rex and what remains of him — fossil fuels, the black gold of many countries upon the face of this wonderful globe. And because black gold, fossil fuels, have become the bargaining chip, what will salvage any country now needing financial help? It is the one product, the one natural resource, that they can use to dissolve their loan, by giving it to the Graymen.

Fossil fuel is here to stay for a while, because there's too much money, power, greed and control involved with it. And what about that which flows from the sun, which is all around you and has been here for quite some time? It has not been technically researched because there is no money in drilling the sun! Are you with me? And anyone can be powered by it; it's not at all elitist. How can you own it? Well, you can't, and that is a great truth.

So fossil fuels, because of the affordability of their control in the world today, are here to stay; and any one individual who takes a stand against them to create any new power sources has heretofore been done away with. Heard you of a term called patents? It's the legitimizing of an idea. Well, there have been many for a very long time that have been put asunder; bought and put away.

However, all is not lost. There is a grand individual in a country called Japan who is indeed a genius of the common people. He has, at this moment, received wondrous technology and science and is developing a folder, that's what it's called, liken unto a book. And through his power source utilizing and storing the sun's energy you could do a fairly good job of running most of your things at home. This entity is very clever and also has a great power that walks with him. This individual will add greatly to social consciousness when all of this is over. Now, no one is going to do away with this entity. No one is going to do away with the enterprise, because the entity has used the system to create his enterprise, very smartly also.

But now, fossil fuels: where would you be without them? Hmmm? How would you get anywhere? On your soles? Pedaling? Or striding a great steed and riding with the wind to get someplace on time? The point is, pilgrims can go around the world in a day. And how marvelous the invention is which allows this; but it's propelled by that which comes from within the Earth. And every person reading this is rather landlocked, property-locked, if indeed they do not utilize this service. Evolution has stopped with fossil fuel.

The Imbalance

What is it doing? Well, at present you have a gaping hole in your stratosphere in your Southern region. It is so large that they won't even write about it any longer. It has grown so large that the researchers are endeavoring to pull out because the radiation coming through that hole is creating cataracts on their eyes. Your atmosphere is the remnants of what once were great seas that surrounded the Earth. It was a great, thick cloud cover. And when water came down and created a more idyllic planet, a very thin, delicate layer continued to cover the Earth and life began to thrive, seasons were born, arid regions were created. And the world truly was a grand and wondrous Eden; Shambala, if you will. And through evolution all sorts of life forms could flourish in this environment, this emerald of the universe.

Now, there was a lot to be said about this in my day, and even prior to my day. Because prior to my time, regardless of what some of your scientists say, there were some very intelligent people who walked this planet. And their source of transportation was light. And in a very small number of years, through some massive quaking in the Earth's exterior, you are going to be able to view some artifacts of that long-gone generation.

In my time, things were not as industrious; that is a great truth. In my time, there was no petrol; that is a great truth. But my times were in harmony with the environment. Certainly my daughter would tease me that my people had B.O. That is the truth; they did. And for the most part, we did not have all of these conveniences that you have that have created broad rumps. Well, that is a truth. And yet, even in my times, man's destiny was to evolve, to become all that he could be. Because life certainly is a gift. This Earth, this sweet endearing planet of yours that is alive, is a gift of creation, and it is designed to evolve to a grander status than even my time knew.

Through the awakening of civilization the forests of every great country have been ravaged. Because of disrespect for the land, its topsoils are gone, its forests are gone, and all the soil can provide is the dust that rides upon a dry, warm wind. And man has moved from those regions to find other regions, not learning from his errors. Though it would seem the Earth was the Lord's, man has taken the Earth for granted, doing whatever he wanted to do with it. And thinking that in his lifetime it wouldn't matter. That is an error.

In every civilization, up to *this* civilization — and I use the term lightly — there has been a raping and plundering of the Earth's resources, as you term them. Actually they are natural elements necessary for life, even the Earth's life. But the most caustic, the most depleting, the most agonizing of civilizations is one bent on high technology and kept in check through greed and power. And the power works all the way to the utilization of fossil fuels.

These tears in your stratosphere were not always there. Certainly the beginning erosion of the stratosphere happened prior to the turning of this, your century, as you call it in your time flow, with the burning of coals, and has continued more rapidly with the discovery of oil.

When you burn fossil fuels without a proper balance on the Earth to take care of the atmosphere, where do you think the remnant goes? Do you think it disappears into space? No. It doesn't go into space. It can only have validity in an atmosphere, so it is held there. In your atmosphere you hold, *even* this moment, the remnants of fires that you burned in your hovels a century ago. Every moment that you start up your engine in your auto machine you send a message to the stratosphere. And where do you think that goes? It disappears and gets out of your face, but where does it go? It goes up and is held there in the belt. Every moment that your technology changes molecular structures and creates chemicals, where do you think that the fumes and by-products of those go? Into the belt. And they are held there. They don't go to the moon. Or to Mars. Or to the sun. They are around your Earth.

Without the proper balance provided by the majestic trees and the foliage of great forests, the dioxins are so severe in the stratosphere that they are now eating away at the lower part of your planet. This has not been addressed as openly as it should be in your media. And why? Because in addressing this issue the media would have to say what is causing the problem. And what is causing the problem is not only freon, but emissions, and chemical wastes: poisons that come off of things and collect in your atmosphere.

What it would mean for anyone to take a stand and say, "We must change this?" It would call into question one of the great industries that your country is based upon: the manufacture of auto machines, internal combustion engines. Who would question the provision of transportation? Who would question the provision of energy to fuel your hovels? There are very few people who are willing to do away with the auto machine and lose their jobs. There are very few people who are willing to do away with fossil fuels. There are very few people who are willing to go without their cool air, artificially created, in order to allow a balance in nature.

Now there are those in your country who have made a great effort concerning this; they are called environmentalists. They are beginning to take all this a wee bit seriously, and they met with major environmentalists from other countries of the world to make a decision to halt the production of freon. But they could not start a decline in production until the end of the century because freon was necessary to the economic growth of up-and-coming Third World countries.

Nature, sweet nature, is really no different than you are in your physical embodiment. The greatest war nature is having to fight at the present time is against the damage being done in its physical embodiment, and that damage is based primarily on fossil fuels. Simple. And yet, fossil fuels have been created as a power tool and a bartering agent — an absolute *necessity* in your country and the world, which cannot easily be given up. But if it were given up, those who are headed for absolute control no longer would have the cat o' nine tails in their hands.

So, what has been done about this? Since the turning of your century, and up until recently, a consortium of entities, which you would not recognize, in the ethers created explosions in your stratosphere, and some of you have seen them. They were brilliant green fireballs. Now, where did they come from and why were they there? For a while no one understood the enigma of these things and what their purpose was.

The purpose was an endeavor to salvage your environment. Some of your brethren — yes, you do have brethren that live on other stars and in another dimension — exploded these green fireballs in your stratosphere in order to help neutralize the effects of the erosion of that stratum. The explosions were quite common. They haven't been happening for quite a while now because it is interference. It has come to the point where you must wake up and become aware of this, your kingdom. The Earth, as it were, is taking measures into its own hands. Hands is probably not the proper term. The Earth is taking measures into its own zippers, yes.

Not only do you have a massive hole above your southern pole; you have one forming in the northern regions. There is one that completely covers the country called Greenland, in Canada, and one forming upon what is termed the Eastern Seaboard. They are quite numerous now; they are forming everywhere because the dioxins are eating away at the substances which create oxygen.

Now, this is really not the best news you would ever want to hear. Because radiation has a direct impact on the delicate ecosystems of your planet. It will deform the fishes of the sea. This will come into the news shortly because there will have to be an explanation for this phenomenon. And they will trace these deformities back to plankton. Hear you of plankton? Indeed, wonderful creatures, plankton. They will determine that the direct radioactivity coming through these holes will deform the plankton and begin to create hybrids that no longer will be able to breed. Plankton is the beginning of the food chain in the sea. Do you understand?

Who Is the Tree Left With?

The Earth, this living organism, has allowed and allowed and allowed. This country that you call your home has been, in many ways, very protected. This is the longest time in recorded history in which a civilization has lived uninterrupted by cataclysmic change. This country, in a sense, has been very protected from many things that have occurred. This country originally was completely self-sufficient for *all* its people, with enough left over for others. You have always had enough available natural resources to take care of your people. It was indeed a great garden — still is, to some extent. But it has been raped and abused and misused through ignorance.

The Earth, understanding this, is experiencing something very dramatic. Every part of its natural environment is crying out. Nature is the breath of life in all things; everything is alive. Just because a tree doesn't talk to you doesn't mean that it does not have an aliveness. It does. A plant is alive. The earth is alive. A great rock is alive. For all things in the kingdom that is called God/Manifest are alive. And all things in nature are crying out; they are in pain.

Now, I could go into this a little more specifically, but if I were to say they are *crying out in pain,* or they are choking, or they are being gassed to death, perhaps that would give you a better understanding of an intelligence that can't speak to you directly. Just like when I spoke about your body with the sores, showering in acid, and smelling poison, and having a continuous bellyache. Well, that is what your wonderful Earth is going through at the present time. It is not without its own ability to change, and it will. The change is already in the process of occurring.

So the Earth and all of nature, those grand dolphins, your brothers, who flung themselves onto the beach and died — they were making a statement. The little animals that pearls of wisdom come from are making a statement too — they are dying. And the fishes that once used to find proper breeding areas which are there no longer are endeavoring to make a statement. Every time a great whale comes upon your shore, it is trying to tell you something. All of this does not go unheard or unheeded. Who is to fend for and take care of life? If man refuses to change, then what is life left with? What is the tree left with? Who is the defender of the porpoise and of the whale? And of the little oyster, whose greatest irritation turned out to be a jewel? Who is the defender of the rocks? The streams? The air? Who has to say for it, "It is your hour; for you shall live, and that which you have spoken will be heard and indeed answered"?

Nature – The Changes

S o NATURE, being a forward-thrust motion called life, has taken
to itself the necessary elements to do something about its own
physical misery. The weather is changing. Yes, you have seen that
now, in hindsight. The earth is moving. The stratosphere has to
heal itself or all of the life forms upon this Earth will not be able
to tolerate the radiation. Simple.

So the Earth is in the throes of great change, more profound
than it has been through since the convulsions of its birth. It has to
make changes in order for it to continue to live.

Fire in the Zippers

Now, movement is happening upon the Ring of Fire. And the
Ring of Fire happens to be a very big zipper that goes all the way
around the world. And it is the dynamics of a process called plate
tectonics. Hear you of that? Now, the activity of the plates, or the
zippers, is what allows the Earth the continuum of evolutionary
progression. For as the plates move into the compressed outward
surface of the Earth, they are changed and transformed and come
up again, renewed, reinvigorated. At the present moment every
continent on the face of your Earth is in movement. They are all
moving, and more rapidly than has ever been recorded before, because the land masses are floating according to the movement of
the zippers, and they are all activated.

Now, the zippers allow a wonderful nutrient to flow from

them — lava — it's recycled earth, and that regenerates and enriches the surface of the Earth for plant life that immediately springs up from it. It is the way that the Earth has of healing its surfaces. And the greatest activity has been, up until this day in your time, in every other place except your country. In the seas there are *violent* volcanoes going off at this very moment, in a desperate effort to purify the water. At the present time there are volcanoes coming to life that supposedly have been dead. Except for the effect on a few of you, all this has been happening to someone else. All of this activity, this *unusual* activity, and it is, is really something that is outside of your own intimate world and your own personal observation of life. It really doesn't relate to what you have to suffer and what you're going to do when you visit your friend. It means nothing to you, because it's not happening to you. But it soon will, because the force that is being pressed against the plates that flow up against your country is more awesome than anything that has ever formed in concealed energy on this plane. And it is ready to move.

The Earth is changing. It is changing also according to man's habitat. For what has been desolate to man before, and therefore not been populated by him, will begin to bloom, and have rainfall, and unusual storm activities that have never been indigenous to the area during man's reckoning. In areas of dense population, as it were, you will begin to see nature reacting more radically to man's involvement. And you will see the natural source of man's thunder change in the days that are coming, very rapidly. *Ancient* places will come alive; ancient volcanoes at this moment are like slumbering tigers.

Why? It's really not to get rid of you, but rather to heal what you've done. And you will see a radical increase in the activity of the Earth moving on all of its zippers from now to the end of this century. In the central cities of business, you will see phenomena occur from within the heavens and under the earth. Cities that are responsible for pollution on your plane will see strange and wondrous things happen in regards to nature and its assaults.

This, the beautiful emerald of the universe, your homeland, will begin to see the thrust of continued change. The hole in the stratosphere, the pressure and the movement upon the zippers, plate tectonics — all this will create a warming effect on your Earth, in the breadbasket of your country, which has been taken over by so many powers who have run the farmer out. The Earth in the next four years will warm up to such an extent that crops will fail in the breadbasket.

Deserts, places where man rarely visits, will be inundated with unusual rainfall. And during this heating up of the world, weather patterns will change. You have seen a little of that even this year in your counting. There is much more to come.

The Earth is progressively endeavoring to do something for humankind, which cares not and renders not for the surface of the Earth. The Earth is endeavoring to move humanity away from its sores, so that it can heal in many places. And those places are very great indeed. Very rarely will you see any changes occurring in areas where there is a balanced ecosystem of nature, where the animals are in harmony with the Earth. Those areas will stay status quo.

The Bittersweet Song of the Flutes

Now, there are two great volcanoes, one in Europe and one sitting on an island in an ocean. And at this moment the activity that is under their flutes is so grand, they are in the process of eruption. Know you that the great famine of Europe, indeed the great famine of Ireland, was the result of one singular volcano that went off in the 1800s that dusted the stratosphere and created winter in the summer, thus freezing all the crops and causing famine? *One* volcano.

There are two at present that are in position to relieve the pressure of the ever-changing plates of this, your planet. On one level the Earth is heating up, and on the other it could cool down. Because if both of these volcanoes decide, at any moment, to relieve that pressure — and only nature decides the moment — with both of them going off into the stratosphere, you are also going to have an immediate cooling of the Earth's surface, which will produce changing, radical weather patterns. If you are living on a zipper, you are taking chances with your life. If you like the zipper and love the view, stay there. If that is the most you can afford, stay there. But you are now in an active zone. If you are living near the water or on the water, you are also in a perilous place, for not only are the known plates moving, but those that are under the sea that not even your scientists are aware of are also moving. And the result is the creation of great waves. It is a natural *reaction* of change.

The Rising Water

Next we must speak of the melting of the polar caps. Have you heard of that possibility? The hole in the stratosphere and the warming up in the next four years is happening much more quickly than your scientists will tell you, and as a result the melting of great caps of snow is already occurring. It will raise the water level two hundred feet, and in the inlet areas in some places only twelve.

The Southern Cap is already melting. The Northern Cap is already in a slow melt, for you have a glacier that has broken off and is now in the water. That is a result of the warming of the water. And it's on the move; there are several of them that are on the move. And it's all right to have a little excess water, but in one glacier *alone,* masters, this country could get its fresh water for the next *thirty* years — that's how great they are.

With the sea level rising as well, it is not well to be upon the water, but to be inland. It is also not well to be in densely populated areas, if you can make the choice for change. The Earth will warm in the next four years, and at any moment, with the eruption of two major volcanoes, you could go into a winter in the middle of summer. The value of crops on an international scale will all be at the mercy of the weather change. For there is one thing that man and his altered ego cannot do, and that is alter the weather and alter the Earth in its changes.

How Would You Feel if Someone Exploded a Nuclear Weapon in Your Navel?

How would you feel if someone exploded a nuclear weapon in your navel? "We are only going to test this, of course, to see how you react!" Do you think that the unleashing of the energy of the weapons of the munitions makers on the interior of the Earth takes place without any repercussions? If you had shock waves going through your belly button, in the center of this country, and the force being created in the interior was being matched equally by the force coming from the ocean due to plate tectonics, you would be in the very direst position, as is your Earth.

And what of your nuclear waste that is being dumped into your fault lines? Do you know the great cavern within that goes up into the Californias? Did you know that nuclear waste has been barrelled up and dumped into the San Andreas Fault? You did not know that? But, of course, how would you? It is a deep cavern; it'll move; the dangerous stuff will get covered up; it'll go even deeper! No. Well, that is what is in the wrinkles of your very Earth: nuclear waste, as it were.

The Earth has a lot to change because it is battling for its very survival. For as the rains come on the Eastern Seaboard and in Europa, the rains of poisons are destroying the natural resources, the forests, and the lands, and the fish, and all life that is dependent on the water.

Where Once There Were Islands

And who is going to stop all this? Do you think that it will be stopped mainly because we are ruining a few trees and destroying a few lakes? If rain that comes down on you is like drinking poison, that's a small price to pay in order to forge forward to complete a dream, a realization, a technology, a civilization. People are really not up to changing — they can't afford to. Between now and the end of this century, many places that are familiar to you today will not even look the same before the end of 1999. And what once were islands will have disappeared. And where there was no land, it will appear. And where once there was desert, thriving saplings will be growing everywhere. And where there were fields of golden wheat, the bread of life, you will find deserts, incapable of sustaining growth.

And nature will react violently in those places where human offal is emptied into the water. And to the abundance of the sea which, in all essence, feeds so many of the people of the world, there is coming a day when fishermen will cast their nets and they will come up with nothing. It is already happening.

You haven't been affected too much by the turbulence of nature and by what is occurring that is now on a roll, because it hasn't really happened in your back yard. You only see pictures of people starving in Africa, and your heart goes out to them; but it really doesn't mean anything to you because you're not the person starving. And it doesn't mean a lot to you when it is not your home that is destroyed when the earth begins to tremble. It happened somewhere else; it was on the news. And though you feel sorry for the people who perished when the earth moved, when mud flowed down from mountains more rapidly than their vehicles could go, though it certainly is a tragedy, it is not really in your reality because it has never really *happened* to you.

The Earth Is On a Collision Course with Humanity

The Earth, in its evolution, in its need to go forward and to sustain itself, is on a collision course with humanity. And humanity, who refuses to listen, who cannot move from their glorious hovels, who cannot miss a sunset over the ocean, who cannot fortify themselves on a piece of land, they are going to find that nature is going to be in violent opposition to them. Yes, it is a truth.

So what about all the people who have moved to the cities, who live on top of one another, who are living in places where there is no earth, no flowers blooming save in artificial pots? Who's going to feed them? Yes, they are the successful, they are the middle class, they are going for more wealth; but who will take care of them, and put the bread upon their tables? Where will it come from? Where is their water going to come from?

In the days that are coming, with the changes in the weather, man has put himself in the most vulnerable position he has ever lived in, for he has moved away from the good earth and is now living in stacks, one upon the other. For humanity, throughout all time and all great changes that have occurred within lifetimes, even in my lifetime, was sovereign enough to go, as you have termed it, *with the flow.* Because humanity, up until now, has lived in *harmony* with its environment, for that is its home.

Look at what you've done for the purpose of civilized humanity, for prosperous humanity, for humanity that lives at the height of its golden age of technology. Man — who can see beyond his immediate moon into the far reaches of space. So what is this humanity that has abandoned the goodness of the earth and moved to fulfill the desires of those who *rule* the Earth?

Arduous times are ahead. Indeed, they are even present at this hour.

There Are Waves Coming That Would Cover Your Tallest Building

To tell you that there are waves coming that would cover your tallest building would mean nothing. It doesn't really mean anything to tell you that whole pieces of land will break off at zipper connections. If I say to you there are great and aristocratic trees dying, it would mean nothing. They are not in your yard! Where would they have to be for you to care? Did you cry from your soul when the dolphins perished on your seashores? What were they telling you? What gentler creatures, though wild and free, could be so affected by the attitude of humanity? You didn't really see them. You just read about it. Some of you cried a river, because you understood in your soul what their death meant to your own being. They will be missed, yes.

The Earth Will Feed You Gladly

Nature is in alignment with the whole of the universe and the whole of forever and ever and ever. A tree will live with you and provide for you shade, shelter, and even food, if you will live in harmony with it. The earth that you sit upon, if love you that earth, will become enriched and will feed you gladly. And the clouds that pass overhead will rain the softest water on you if you are in *alignment* with them, if you respect them. For how else could humanity have survived for eons, unless it had not been for a splendid few who understood what could never have been spoken, but could only be lived?

Nature Is On the March

But now nature is on the march. Listen, it is not because God hates you — that's the victim crying out. It is not because the world hates you — it doesn't hate, only man hates. This isn't your penance for not being do-gooders. It is evolution. This is change. And remember when I spoke to you about whose side to take in all this and I said I wouldn't take sides against the Graymen at all? That is because only nature in its thrust has the power and the mobility to disrupt the whole plan.

And I want you to know there is a lot in the unseen that is aligned with your precious Earth. And that which is aligned with nature is in alignment with the God Within, the Without, the All that IS in the All. And while industry continues to go forward and countries become faceless and the world order begins to take nice, tidy shape, the Earth is saying, "*Enough.*"

When You See in the Papers that the Water Is Rising, Bless It

So when see you in the papers, if you're fortunate, that the water is rising, bless it. When you hear of a great fiery volcano going off, bless it. That is letting the steam off and is allowing the regeneration of nature through the plates and their movement. Now the next moment that you hear of storms, bless them. They are there to assure a continuum.

Courage and Grace
Are Required

I N MY LIFE I thought the grandest thing that I had ever seen was
the sun — the grandest thing. And the second grandest thing
was the moon, and things that happened *out "there."* Without
these life forces, the tenuous human being, so easily bruised and
cut and hurt, would not have a home to express in. The sun is not
there to sear you; it is not there to hurt you. It is there to promote
your life.

Did You Know There Are Universes
where the Sun Is Blue?

You know, there are universes where the sun is blue. Did you
know that? *Blue* lights instead of yellow lights; yours is very
unique — a yellow sun. And through photosynthesis you have the
extraordinary color called green. Did you know that green is not
seen in other places? It's a different color. It's not green. But
because you have a yellow sun, you have the color green on your
planet. That is what makes it so wonderful, so unique, and indeed
the home of Gods, who have sort of taken it for granted up to
this point.

Until a Host Appears in the Heavens (and They Are On Their Way)

When? It's already happening. How soon? Tomorrow? The evolution of these changes will go on until the end of this century, until a host appears in the heavens. And they are on their way. And what does this mean? It means that in the last days of the age of tyrants a power will be unleashed that is uncontrollable by people whose whole idealism up to this point was to collapse the vacuum of choice to create complete enslavement. And this power will work harmoniously to allow the meek to indeed inherit the Earth.

Listen to the Tree, It'll Talk to You

And what do you think you are, out here? To say you are the meek does not mean that you are a simple-minded idiot. The meek are entities that gain knowledge by listening to nature — listen to the tree, it'll talk to you — understand which way the wind is blowing and move accordingly; they are the meek. They are actually the ingenious, for they survive it all.

You can't go on tearing up the stratosphere. Without nature intervening this would become a society that would live much like my original peoples lived, in a place long forgotten, a very controversial place, Lemuria. Because my people lived underground because of all of the animals above the ground.

Without nature intervening you would not be able to walk out into your sunlight. And even in the year coming up and the years to come, there will be a radical increase in the sores on people whose skin is exposed to the sun. And why in this country? Because there is a hole appearing above. It is small, but it is expanding. And if this went unchecked, the whole world would be ruled by the elite underground, and the workers would stay above ground, and that would be your lot in life. But it's not going to happen, because that is not the outcome held in the palm of the Almighty.

Have the Courage and Grace Within to Make the Changes Necessary to Ride Out the Storm, Because There Is One Brewing

You, whose eyes are challenged by these words, I want you to remember something. The reason you don't change is because you are afraid of what you will be in the unknown and of what lies there, because it is not identifiable. This is one change you should never fear. But have the courage and grace within you to make the changes necessary to ride out the storm, because there is one brewing. And those changes are pertinent, not only on an economic level, but literally on a survival level. Seemingly, the burger places will never run out of burgers. And there will always be a lot of bread on the shelf, won't there? You can choose. And if it's a day old, you can throw it away; there will be more! Won't there? No — because the whole living pattern of foodstuffs is changing.

So it would seem that you are pitted against two great forces. Again, I would line up with nature if I were you. The other seems very pleasurable because it's that comfort zone — it's the box. It's the card. Seemingly, that is your ticket to a more comfortable life. But I want you to know that the troubled times that are coming are not without hope.

A world is coming that survives the ending of this age. And it is made up not of Graymen, and not of those who give up their ability for freedom because they choose to, but of those who have been termed and prophesied to be the radical few of God. And there are many of you reading these words who will see all of these times.

So now, what to do about all of this? Well, again, your future is indeed about choices, which I cannot make for you. I can give you the options; you have to make the choice. I cannot choose for you any more than I can grow for you; you have to do that on your own. But there are choices coming for you to make, and you will become more aware of them in the next fortnight and in the days to come than you were ever aware before. And they are not horrible, and they're not nasty, and they're not mean — they are just choices. They shouldn't be reacted upon out of fear but rather by obtaining the knowledge to survive. Get it?

Who Will Feed You when Your Farmers Have Been Conspired Against?

If you are in the city, you can choose to stay where you are. And if you choose not to leave the city, I ask only that you do this. Take your gold that you would party upon, and party by putting it into extensive foodstuffs and water. If you have to stay in the city, I would ask you to be prepared. You are going to have to have foodstuffs. I am not telling you this just because I like to hear myself give you a gloomy forecast, but because it is a natural fact. Because who will feed you when your farmers have been conspired against? Their food has been left to rot in the fields, in order to promote other countries. And the food that you are buying, you are buying from other countries, rather than from your own farmers. And who is going to feed you? Because the weather change is worldwide.

Find a Piece of Land and Love It; It Will Love You Back

If you desire to sustain yourself and you live in the city, then move from where you are. But make the choice because it *feels* in you to be the important thing to do. Find yourself a piece of land and love it; it will love you back. And there create your hovel, whether it be a palace or a lean-to. Yes, a lean-to under a tree. That is all right as long as it is your land; do this to gain your sovereignty. And of your *In God We Trust* dollars? In the days to come you should invest in gold. For it has sustained a three-thousand-year-old barter system. And, in the final analysis, it will be the only thing that will have the value to buy your sovereignty completely when the transfiguration occurs from paper and economic monies to *one* card.

After the initial major plunge, your market will rally, of course, and many people will make some paper money off of your taxation. I want you to know something about the elite. They do not pay taxes. And another thing: their dollars are tied up in safe places. They have *never* paid taxes. But *you* will, as it is seen this moment.

Playing in Illusions

And so, as a result of some people's gain off the plunge, the market will look wonderful and preferable, but the gain will be at your expense! I want you to understand that. There are greater things to apply one's capital funds to than intangibles. Because when one plays the gambling game, he is playing in illusions, and someone pulls the strings to those illusions. Tangibles are what will fortify you in all of the times coming. Your sustenance and your freedom will depend on whether you have a piece of land that you call your own, that will be your own throughout all of the turbulence that will come; in that land you will have, through the God within you, a shelter, and you will be seen through all things that are coming.

Tangible. The land. The good earth. You never really own the land. It is there for you to use. It is your home in this experience. But it will be there as long as you use it. It will fortify you. It will feed you. It will support you. And the gold will pay off your indebtedness, so that no one owns you. And with your foodstuffs you will survive, because after this day everything that is seen in the moment will become erratic. And the flow will become cluttered and at any moment things will occur, because after this day you will be living in an erratic world — nature has declared war.

The Graymen are struggling. They are endeavoring to keep the plan suppressed, but *blessed* be the person who has spoken out the truth. And there are many speaking the truth who have never heard of Ramtha. And some people are waking up.

Let the food fortify you through all of the upcoming changes. And this country will be a radical nation in the last days. This will be a radical nation of a radical people, who will rise up against their enslaver. That will come in this land. And the greatest message will come from the Great Northwest.

Now, who's going to win the war? The side of the light. It is in destiny. That is the choice. And nature is aligned with the light. To sustain is to own your power, to own your place, to fortify your body. It is to become sovereign and to learn to attend to the needs of, yes, being even simple people. There is nothing wrong with that. And I would advise you not to take the mark of the beast, the debit card, though you may choose to do whatever you desire to do; for it is your will to choose. It is not absolute law in the world yet. It is subtly being manipulated there.

How long will this take? The whole economies of the money system have to fall, worldwide, for the debit card to be implemented as the salvation. You have four years, as it is seen at this moment, to sustain your fortune and indeed your sovereignty; to be able to exchange with the dollar so you can create complete sovereignty. For four years, as it is seen at this moment according to the people who govern the world, is the optimum date to accomplish their goal. There is a lot that will happen in four years!

Now, days to come? Well, we have talked about the economy and why it is the way it is. We have talked about the Earth and its changes and why it is necessary for it to change. And we have talked a bit about choice, and why you are divine to make those choices.

Remember I said to you, there is hope? Yes? Remember I said there are options? Yes? Those who possess true understanding as free people have extraordinary options. Those who gain absolute sovereignty, and live within the perimeters of their land, and remain independent of the broader economic community, have many options open to them.

There are a lot more of you who have this information than will read this book. There are many in countries other than your own who also are aware of these things. Do you think that the greatest financial wizards have their farms, and their wells, and their monies buried in gold and silver coins just because that happens to be a freaky habit of theirs? They are not some poor slobs who are listening to some outrageous character tell them all of these things that are coming about. These are entities who are aware; they have already made provisions. Where do you think the Graymen are going? They live in *mountains*. They have refuge. Certainly they have their palaces, but they have their safe places. Do you think that they do not think that there is the possibility of a failure? Oh, they are prepared very nicely.

So, is this simply a learning experience for a bunch of spiritual people following an outrageous entity somewhere? Not at all! It is only through the rise of such altered egos that humanity has left the earth, their land, and congregated into grand cities and become the slaves of those who own them. And it is only recently that humanity ceased growing and harvesting their own food, and putting provisions away. Today, with all of your conveniences, it must seem rather silly to store food. But it is a wise person who is doing it. And many of the wise ones know not of what I am, and know not of you; and many of them are very well educated and are very aware of what is coming to pass.

Why Hasn't the Cosmos Said, "Hey, You, Wake Up"?

Now, you're not alone out here, so why hasn't the cosmos said, "Hey, you, wake up"? Indeed, why haven't your brethren who are in the great and fiery ships spoken to humanity? Why hasn't God, the Great Thought, talked to you? Why is everyone keeping silent on the subject? There will not be silence much longer. Because every part of everything is the All In All. The Is, God, the Mother/Father Principle, has kept silent and allowed the reflection of what this is about — the human drama — so that mankind has been able to experience an unfolding through the will that is given to them. So that you may come forward by choice, to become God/Man/Woman realized. And it has allowed — allowed.

Imagine Space Having a Voice!

So the Great Thought — imagine space having a voice! — has said nothing aloud. You've heard of angels. Well, there are a lot of different angels. There are some that are entities of a higher vibration, a higher energy mass. And then there are those angels of old that appeared to peoples of this Earth and gave them prophecies and tried to lift them out of their negligence. And those angels come in great ships. They are the fiery forms, the fiery ships, and they are henceforth going to be more visible in your skies.

If You Think that You Are the Only Splendid Thing in This Universe, You Are More Narrow-Minded than I First Perceived

And more people are going to have contact with these beings. More and more and more. They *do* exist. If you sit there and think that you are the only splendid thing in this universe, you are more narrow-minded than I first perceived. And if you think that out of ten *billion* suns in the Milky Way — and in those suns whole universes exist — if you think that this emerald with its yellow sun on the outermost part of the mind of God is the only stage that plays the human drama, you need a vision. I will send you one. So be it!

They Have Managed to Warp Time for Their Own Convenience

You have brothers and sisters with human intelligence out there. Yes, they look different than you do. That is because their environment is different. Remember? The blue sun and no green? There are different systems, and the very environment changes the human being. But that doesn't make them less beautiful and less loving. And it does not mean they don't have souls, because they do. These entities have played a great part in your evolution.

Remember, you are in a very slow time flow. They have managed to warp time for their own convenience. That's the intelligence that awaits in Superconsciousness.

Now, these entities are very aware of what is going on here. They are very aware of the destruction of the tissue of the Earth. They are very aware of the stratosphere. They are very aware. Why should they be aware? Because they are your brothers and sisters, and your father is indeed their father. And they are the angels of old that appeared unto your past humanities. They were the angels who gave the vision of Revelations. Yes, they moved the spirit of prophets to speak. To all countries. It was not only to Abraham and his people, but to peoples before him, to help bring humanity out of its stagnation and into its evolution!

They Are Not Coming to Gulp You All Up and Take You Away to Someplace Else

And they are not here to save you; they are here to help you. They are not coming to gulp you all up and take you away to someplace else. Why would they want to do that? They have their own environments to think about! Well, it is a truth. Look what you've done to yours. Why would they let you loose on theirs?

They are here to help salvage the Earth. They are in alignment with its movement and its motion. They are also here as intimidators, to intimidate the grand spectrum called the altered ego. They are here to stop the war against the radical few of God. And their fire will be like a scorpion from the sky. They are here to help those who will not tolerate the robbing of their liberty, ultimately their freedom, and to press those who would collapse the vacuum. They are on your side.

It Is Finished

And they are working in harmony with the Earth and its movement, and to change the pressing of the economy and the ultimate enslavement of the world. They are working for one singular voice that has never, ever, been heard. The Voice of God. The Voice that comes from all things, from the furthermost star, from beyond the vision of what you think space is, through all the levels of all the universes, a voice which speaks the words that have never been spoken — and the words are, "It is finished."

The End of Time

That sounding is the final release of the altered ego. And yes, how can the flourishing of humanity continue when what has been in the continuum, the ability — God-given — to have a will, to make change, and to make choices, no longer exists? Don't you understand? When you give away your choice — indeed to no longer have a choice, but to be owned — it is the end of time. Remember now, time, which is manifested destiny, is based on choice and collective attitude which is experienced in this now, and which assures the future.

And when the future no longer contains choice, but has been collapsed into a mass of humanity who have given away their power *completely,* then there is no more evolution in the human drama, the human spirit. For what would life be without choice? Indeed, what would evolution be? What would the spirit revel in? Where would be the *wild* freedom of the soul? And what could it evolve into? Would it perish and come back again into a soul that has given away its power completely? That is what the debit card means.

The card, as it is termed, is not evil. It is merely the instrument. It is the instrument by which you give away your inalienable right to freedom, indeed your divine right of choice to be a living, vital individual, a human being glorified in the bosom of the forever and ever and ever. And time is at an end. Don't you understand that this is what is meant by the end of time?

Time is only relevant to change. It is only relevant to evolution. Evolution doesn't need to exist if there is no time. And yet time and evolution are one and the same thing. They are in the flow; they must coexist together — life, continuum. And when you no longer evolve, and when you no longer have choice except through the instrument, you have made the choice to give away your divine right for individualism and manifested destiny. Get it?

What Be the Labor and the Land if There Is No Freedom?

So what are — and this teaching gets more outrageous by the sentence — so what are your great brothers endeavoring to do? To give the choice of the continuum to you, the radical few; because, after all, what is an anvil or a plough to them? What be the labor and the land, if there is no freedom? It means nothing. And humanity involved in the drama of this understanding has yet to realize the grandest potential of the Christ that is within, of the *nobleness* of mankind and womankind. You have yet to understand what you can do without the altered ego. You have yet to realize what you can be without limitation. That is why there is intervention; that is why it is necessary for nature to move. That is why *they* are coming to help you.

Do you know that you already know? Do you know that you make the choices without knowing it? That is what this book is about. In reading this book you are gaining the knowledge that allows you to make the choice. You can have the instrument, the card, but you will have sold your soul. Or you can deny the instrument and live off the coddling of the Earth that will take care of you. And by that decision you will be known, even by your greater brothers; they will know, in these times that are a-coming.

And Without the Instrument, the World Order Cannot Track Your Movements. Think About It!

I told you that there would never be a nuclear war — that is truth. Even the Graymen can't really afford one. What would be the use of blowing everything up if you want to be the ultimate authority? So what are the days of fire that are coming?

Fire. A lot has to do with the changes in the Earth; fires raging out of control on the surface of the Earth. Yes, they are coming; they have already been here; they will continue. What does it mean, as it were? From the moment the radical few of a radical nation stand up and say, "Enough. We shall not do this," global war *will* ensue upon this land for the first time ever. And the war will be waged with threats of nuclear annihilation. They own the toys.

It is when the Graymen threaten, it is then that the voice will be heard: "It is finished."

The Whole Is Affected
by the One

A ND YOU WILL look up into the heavens and see an armada beyond imagination, that is there on the side of you that have so chosen, for it is known who you are. And the champions of the human drama will emerge. And there are many of them who aren't in this audience. They are other places. They know this innately. They have allowed themselves to be aware to know it. They have become greater than their fears. They know it. They are known as well. There are people in other countries that know it as well. How did they know? They just knew. Because the Lord God of Their Being, that has indeed endeavored to live courageously, showed them. They know. So there are more; more than will ever see this book. There are many, many more.

By the Year 2042, the Earth Will Again Look Like It Did when I Knew It

So what will come? Well, your brothers will help you clean up the stratosphere. They know how to do it. Through re-seeding and stabilization of its movement and weather patterns, the Earth, by the year 2042, will again look like it did when I knew it. Growth will be lush and life will be green, skies blue and water clean; that is its destiny. And it will heal itself. It is already seen. It is set in destiny. That is how it is. It is law. So be it!

83

He Is Returning

In this host that is returning, Yeshua ben Joseph, Jesus, Manifest Christ, lived and still does. For that entity, *blessed* entity, manifested God as God living through man. There have been lots of beliefs concerning this great Christ. And that is not a point of argument, except that he still lives. And the entity endeavored to teach that what was within him is within you. And he promised to return. He is returning, in the armada. The entity, Yeshua ben Joseph, is a manifested God that had the angels at his beckoning, and I am speaking of seen and unseen entities. Because he had the expanded all-knowingness to be aware of them; what you do not see, he saw, and still does.

The resurrection of the Christus — which means God/Man, indeed, God/Woman realized — is Christ coming back to absolve what has been called a devil, that which is called the altered ego; to absolve it and go forward with the divine plan of man — to create, to choose, to live, to fortify the continuum. The second coming is not outside of you. It is not out there. It is within. The Battle of Armageddon is within. It is the battle of your Christ within, coming forward to take back its rightful place within, thus defeating the altered ego of man. Your altered ego is the Antichrist. The Antichrist is not outside of you. It, too is within. And that is the battle, the fight between your own Christ and your own Antichrist.

But the entity known as Yeshua ben Joseph will return as well. Yes, and many other great entities will return, for they are in a timeless flow. Now this is not told to herald anyone's revelation, nor is it told to scare anyone. It is simply telling it like it is. For the moment the voice is sounded that comes from all parts of all life to say, "It is finished. Behold! It is done," whole dimensions will open up and the vitality of the human experience will have an opportunity to grow through the grandness of the kingdom within.

Those Who Have Lived for the Glory of God Within Them Will Rejoice

An entire armada is already on its sojourn. You will see more and more of them, as I have promised, in your heavens. And one day the whole host will be seen in the skies. And those who have lived for the glory of God within them will rejoice. For that which they always knew inside will be out in the open; that which they had always experienced and suspected — the unseen God they talked to — will be revealed.

And as for the God that everyone thought must be someone's imagination? They'll hear the Voice of All Life as it reverberates in the last days. But the last is the beginning of the new.

This time of change, this precipitous waltz of the tyrants will have come to a close. The radical last days of this tyranny and the human experience — war and death created for the purpose of control — will nevermore be experienced in the human realm. The message of the Days To Come will affect *all* of your lives, no matter how little you contemplate what you read here or how greatly you consider it.

For what you are reading here this day is the living word, and the living word will manifest. You will become aware of these things as they materialize in your environment. Rejoice with them. It means an end to sorrow and despair and war and death and disease. Hate and bitterness will be finished. For those are the emotions of the altered ego — the Antichrist. So be it!

I desire for you to know that I love you greatly. Outrageous as all of this sounds, it is the truth. Unbelievable. Unpractical. Unusable. *"Raining on my parade."* But it is the truth that will set you free, forever and ever and ever. You only have to look at your own life to see how your altered ego has integrated itself. You only have to see what the effects of an altered ego out for power can be in the small, intimate world of yourself. And if you can see it clearly in your own life, then why is it not feasible on a worldwide scale? It is.

And listen, another thing that I endeavored to impart to the lot of you is that you are divine. Yes, you are. Even your excrement, it is divine, because it is life. There is nothing vulgar or nasty about life. It is an opportunity, a grand opportunity, to live, to see a sunrise, to reflect in the full moon. But it has been an arduous task, to say the least, endeavoring to get past your altered egos so the message that you are divine could go within, where it could be lived.

I have taught you and endeavored to stretch you in so many ways. Whatever worked, I did. I did whatever it took to rattle your box, to jolt you out of your lethargy, so you could see something important, something that you affect, all of you. The things I told you about when I first addressed you regarding Change and The Days To Come has already been documented — it has come to pass. So will this. And as it is seen at this moment all of this is still coming, whether through human design or nature's reaction to it.

You Are the Virtue of Your Choices

Try to say "I love God," and to say "I am divine." Say "I love God" and let that whole statement reverberate inside of you. What is your life in the light of all eternity? How do your choices seem in the light of all eternity, in this *breath* of life of yours, in these few moments? What is it worth to say, "Yes, that which is the without is within me and I am divine"? You are the very virtue of your choices — that is a grand statement, but it is the truth.

There is nothing that I have addressed, and I just skimmed the surface, that one who is endowed with a divinity cannot change. In the next moment if three of the Graymen, and I must use that term because it does fit, suddenly saw the light, they alone would wreak havoc with the rest of the plan. Don't you think the light is being pressed to them? Absolutely!

Don't you know that addressing the lawmakers with this information, as it is seen this moment, is the graceful way to allow them an option to change? They are Gods. They are endowed with divine light, just as you are.

Don't you know that this is manifested destiny, to address you in your decisions? That to tell you what is seen this moment gives you the right to change your mind? Do you understand? Now that you know, you can do something about it.

The whole is affected by the one. Yes, it is. And these people have you by the jugular when it comes to money; they do. But don't you think they are loved? They are. As it is seen this moment; this moment is steadfast in what I have told you this day. Cities will rock and they will crumble. People will be herded into one consciousness. They will be intimidated. And the Earth will continue to roll.

How Great Are You?

Don't you know that in the next moment — which is the future — all of this could change? Yes. But how great are you? Are you willing simply to change enough to provide provisions for yourself? If you cannot bring yourself to see the necessity in that, then what makes you think that mankind as a whole could change his use of fossil fuels, regardless of the fact that it is destroying the Earth? If you can't see the need to put up your own food, why should they see the need to cease their greed? Fair? Yes, it is.

The Greatest Thing You Can Do for Humanity Is to Say, "No, Thank You."

And yet change takes a lot of courage. It takes courage to reject a future that was so planned out with success, money, fame, and the recognition of doing something historic for humanity. Let me tell you something that may shock you. The greatest thing you can do for humanity is to say, "No, thank you." Not what you had expected, is it? Not what college and parents and the system had programmed for you?

So, what about your tomorrow? This information will affect a lot of futures. And yet, the future is only as strong as the moment lived. The more the awareness comes to the surface in enlightenment, knowledge and understanding, the greater your chance of waking up and surviving. Look at those fish that are lying on the beach. What are they telling you? Look at the tree. Why is it dying? It only takes a moment to wake up. And as more and more people wake up, the whole of the world could change the next moment. Do you understand? For certainly nature is on your side, and that is a most compatible relationship, as long as the respect and regard for life is there.

You Have the Power to Plant a Seed

I love you, masters, for I have been one of you. And even this hour, as you read my words, I address you in what certainly would be considered an unusual expression.

Remove the guardian from the door, set your altered ego aside, let your judgments go and hear these words. You have the power to change your personal reality, to bring joy to your expression. You have the power to plant a seed and watch wheat grow. You have the power to make the difference, but it takes courage to make that difference.

You are not reading this to get anything but information about your future. You want to know what's happening. You want to know what's going to happen. You picked this book up to understand. That took courage, but the greatest courage comes from God within you, not from your altered ego. And that great courage is aligned specifically with the forward thrust called evolution/nature/life. It takes courage to look after yourself. It takes courage to live your light, that your light may be brilliant to the world. It takes a rare entity to live like that. But there are entities reading this passage that are just rare enough and just outrageous enough to be that light. Because they want to.

Dignity. There is no dignity in enslavement — there never was.

The only dignity is in a human being who is free and is sovereign. That is what human dignity is about. And the sovereign man is one who lives his dignity to the greatest of his ability in his own intimate world throughout the whole of all eternity.

No one got you in this pickle. No one forced humanity to be in this condition. You rather slid into a comfort zone that made it all right. It was a deception that created a veil of security. It was allowance, and it was not taking responsibility for your personal life. It was giving the responsibility to governments, politicians, and kings; to money-makers, to bankers. You gave them the power to make the decisions about what your world should be like. And if it isn't right, you can always blame them! But it begins with *you,* and who you are.

What You Have Created You Can Uncreate

Sovereignty is nearly lost. It is almost a mythical dream, something not really tangible in this world of cold, hard facts and realities. But yet, it is the optimum for each entity to achieve in this understanding. What you have created you can uncreate, by getting unstuck and going forward. And yes, that could mean living off of your land, in a hovel, and growing your own food. If that means making as much gold as you possibly can in the next four to five years and embracing genius every chance you get, to buy your freedom, to secure your right, then go for it. I'll help you. So be it!

Every Boring Thing in Your Life Is a Repetition of the Altered Ego

It means taking back your dignity and your power. That is what it means to live from the God of Your Being, rather than the altered ego. If it means coming forward for the first time in your life and growing hair, do it! If it means taking charge of your life, do it! If it means changing and moving forward, then go forward.

If it means you must realize that every boring thing in your life is a repetition of the altered ego, something already learned and yet repeated, then realize it! And go forward.

Only in a Bold Assertion Is Genius Born

And it may well mean, for the first time in your life, that you speak from the Lord God of Your Being, and boldly speak a truth. And it may mean that perhaps everyone will despise you because you say it, but you will have become an individual! And you won't need to give away anything. You won't need to betray anyone to love God. You need not ever prostitute anything to man for the love of God. And yet only in a bold assertion and move is genius born.

Is there a great light that walks with you? Is there the opportunity that allows you? Are you chosen? For the faceless mob will not be chosen, for they have made their choice not to make a choice.

When Forgiveness Is Not the Fashion

How subtle can living your own integrity be? Isn't it hypocritical to be outraged at the hole in the stratosphere and then get in your auto machine and fire it up and go for a drive? Living your own integrity is as subtle as being steadfast about something that you know is right within you, and having the boldness and courage to live it. It can be as subtle as making the choice to show kindness in a society that favors indifference. Perhaps it is choosing forgiveness when the fashion is not to forgive.

And perhaps it is for you to say, "Within my reality I have no enemies. For within my reality exists only the glory of God. And in the glory of God omnipresent lies not evil, but the continuum of forever good. And thus is my reality. For it is within the hearts of men that wickedness and war are chosen. In mine, I choose those expressions no longer. I have no enemies."

As bold as that. That is living a truth that is reflected onto *all* of the fabric of life. Spiritual mumbo-jumbo doesn't do anything if it's not lived and not recognized as the heartbeat of life itself. A philosophy will only gain you a lot of talk and a lot of repeating. It will have no relevance to putting bread on the table. All of the crystals in the world — you can live in them, wear them, serve on them, sit on them, sleep on them, travel with them — they will not make you survive. And they will not allow you to know God. That is personal.

Everything that is changing is volatile. Everything that is occurring can be changed in the next moment. The whole human race has had no recent ideals, only hypocrites. But the ideal was never anything outside of yourself, but rather *you* yourself. Get it?

As I have told you, you already chose what has been chosen. And if you now make changes and choose to live in what will be criticized as a stupid, outrageous, inconceivable, uncompromising way of life, and yet if that way of life affords you liberty and sovereignty, then forgive your brother who criticizes you, for he is merely echoing the sentiments of those who own him.

And if you choose to be the Lord God of Your Being, you will see the glory of God and hear the voice that has never been heard. You will see the return of the immaculate Christ, and many like him. You will see the Lord of Hosts. You will see the New Jerusalem, the *New Age* as it is so termed. But really you will see Superconsciousness. And with the removal of the altered ego, the brain opens and blooms. With the removal of fear, the soul is in evolution. With the removal of the blinded cataracts of limitation, you will be able to see the dimensions and light that you've never perceived before. You will even see me.

How close are all of these things? Your financial market will be erratic from this point forward. It is set to fall; it has been planned to fall; that is on the agenda.

Your gold will not always be available to you. If you purchase it, purchase it as soon as you can. No matter what you are paying for it, it will buy your sovereignty in the days to come.

To those who labor, your economy is changing, and many of the hopes and dreams and aspirations of middle-class America are not going to be realized. And yet there is a greater way to realize them, not through the love of money, but through the love of God within you and the power to manifest them. You will be helped. And if you have not gotten your foodstuff, I would advise that you save it up, though you may choose differently. Food is growing everywhere at present. It is fundamentally plentiful, especially in the Northwest. Take advantage of what is now, for the now is subject to change. And, of your water — dare say I there are a few reading this who have already experienced a small hint of what it could be not to have water — it is imperative. And the land is imperative.

And if you don't have the ways and means to procure these things, and yet you have the desire and the need to change, you will be helped. And if you have love for one another, *help* one another. And if you have no land and yet your brother has plenty, ask him to grow your garden there and you tend to it. It will be made manifest. And if you say you know nothing of this, I will send you the runners who will help you learn — if you make the choice.

And if you say, "This is certainly not happening in the prosperous means that I had hoped it would," hang on. Things are volatile. Again, what is it worth for you to gain the whole world and to, indeed, lose your soul, which means to have sold your divine right for choice to gain what only seems like the world? You will die. And in the last breath your one greatest fear will be realized — someone else is gonna get what is yours! Yes!

Now, what I have told you in regards to the Graymen and some of the history of your Earth certainly has not been in-depth, for there are greater things I can talk about and will talk about in paragraphs yet to come.

But I will tell you this. I am pressing an energy toward you, aligned with the Lord God of Your Being, so that in the time that is left for great choices to be made, when you make choices that follow your truth, you will become very prosperous, but in such a way that you are not purchased by that prosperity. Do you understand what I mean by that? Because you are gamblers by nature, and gambling in the soul means to lose. If it meant to win, they wouldn't call it gambling. Get it?

When You Embrace Courage, You'll Have It.
When You Embrace Fear, You'll Get It.

And with this energy, you will have the momentum to be able to make the changes that will help you meet your needs. But you have to make your choices first, and they cannot be spawned by fear. They must be spawned from God Within You, because this is right. And only then will you not be the victim. If you do it any other way, you will victimize yourself.

How do you get rid of fear? Choice. You choose to be afraid. You choose to be a victim. And you choose not to have courage — it's that simple. When you embrace courage, you'll have it. When you embrace fear, you'll get it.

And I do not want, above all, to have you in what is called the pits. Because I do not want to depress you, I want to educate you, so that you will have a broader understanding — so when you look out the window you will know what is coming.

There is only one place in your world where war is really occurring. All the other "wars" are perpetrated, created for the purpose of bringing forth the call of democracy, which brings forth the loans to cover the costs, which brings forth the selling of the people's wills. The countries that are truly at war with one another at the present time have nothing to do with this manipulation, but are about something that is very primeval.

The things I want you to consider as you study these words are the world economy and the hole in the stratosphere. That is what is happening to your Earth. And that is what we are looking at here. I wanted you to know. Not to strain you or make you cower in the face of it, like a little child, but so that you consider it with a maturity in spirit that will allow you to understand this, so that you're no longer in ignorance. Because they'll never tell you how it is until it is finished.

Now, I only sent you a couple of runners in this text, runners being persons who help you see something, or an opportunity, a vision. One I am sending you is a vision, for those who don't think life exists anyplace else. And I have called upon the fiery ships to manifest before you, so that you can see them — two small runners. I did not manifest any of your fears; I figured you were dealing with enough of that without any additional help from the unseen. And I am not manifesting your choices for you, because you will have to address those, and determine your own truth, and pick your own way to go.

So the runners were very skinny in this update; I didn't get a lot of them. But the visions and the experiences that you are going to be getting as a result of this journey will be unforgettable.

What I do impart to you in this book is the courage that comes forth from this beloved body that I occasionally borrow. It takes courage on her part to allow this information to come forward, for it is the truth. And that is a very courageous and daring thing to do. And yet there is nothing that will happen to this house. For I am strong at the door of this house.

Only with an understanding of these things will my brethren and the radical few of God be able to choose who they are and where they are now. And with the information given here, and an understanding of this information, you will be able to make those choices to the glory of God, the Father that is within, and to the glory of that which is coming.

Reviewing all of this was not really difficult at all. The hard part is knowing you are struggling with what you are reading. I see your disbelief at this incredulous information — not only is my existence incredulous to some of you, but what I am saying to you is incredulous. And I know how completely disagreeable all this is and how hard it has been to allow it to come into your reality. I am watching you struggle with it.

I want you to know something. It takes a warrior, very much like the inner being, to have the courage to go forward in any situation. Only when you're namby-pamby do you lay down and wimp yourself into a silent death because someone calls you on the carpet about it and tells you, "You aren't made of the right stuff!"

Well, all of you are, and when I put this knowledge out there, right in front of your eyes, I watch you struggle with it. I know who is suffering, who is outraged, and who understands completely. I know who are the fanatics, and I know who are the realists. And I know from watching you struggle as you read this just how severe the pain of all this is to your being, but I also know that it is necessary that you have this realization to spur your life into change so you can survive it all!

This isn't a question of going out and dying for your country. Do you know how many people *died* for their country? They really didn't have to *die* for their country. They died for someone else's deals, someone else's contrived bargains, and someone else's dream of control. This is not a question of that. But it is a question of addressing what is real in the world and what a truly free person is really like. You can say, "Yes, I'm free. I have a *very* large savings account." Is that what you call them now? Savings accounts. You don't bury it any more? You give it to the banks — definitely a safe place.

Grow Fat and Lay with the Good Woman

So, you have all of that, do you? You have a nice retirement for when the old soldier no longer wants to march, and you can grow fat and lay with the good woman. Got no bills. You can do pretty much what you want to do. You think that's sovereign? But complete sovereignty is truly having what you have absolutely, owning it, and not being owned by anyone. People used to live like that, and not too far removed from your immediate future you will live that way again.

And I see you struggle with that, and what that means to your comfort zones that you've worked so hard for all of your life. You must know this: your government is failing you, because your government is owned *outside* of the government. And I know the pain that brings you. I did not come to hurt you. But perhaps in the pain you'll rise up and make the proper decisions for your life, for the sake of you in your continuum. This I desire.

So, in addition to the slim runners, the vision and the manifested fiery ships, the greatest thing I desire you to reap from this book is the information. I came to point out the state of the world and have you take a look at it, and to tell you the "why" behind the state it is in. So that when things happen, you don't blame God and you don't blame the Earth. So when the storm rolls in and the Earth splits open, you don't feel like a victim. Because if you've been a victim of anything, it has been of your own superstition and ignorance.

Spiritual truth doesn't belong to a bunch of unseen entities and a bunch of bizarre practices. Spiritual truth happens to be everything. To separate one's spiritual truth from his way of life is hypocritical. And those who live in hypocrisy live in a duality. And those who live in a duality repeat that duality lifetime after lifetime. And they end up finding life a rather boring experience, but they live it through and through, over and over.

If You Have the Courage to Walk Forward, I Will Be the Wind at Your Back

The one last thing I will tell you in this segment is that I am not going to abandon you, even in the unseen. For I am a great trumpeter of truth here, and I stand alone in what I have to say; for I will see you through all of this, every moment as it manifests. And I know who is playing monkey business and who isn't. And whichever of you stands up, whether it is a subtle rising of spirit or whether you come to full realization in a moment; if you have the courage to walk forward, I will be the wind at your back. I promise you. For I have not created this book just to give you information and then leave you high and dry. There is a purpose to this madness, and that is to see you through all of these times. But I will not help those who refuse to help themselves.

You have a great power that is with you. And one day, when you look up, you will realize just how great it is. And perhaps on the day you see that greatness, you can also see the greatness in yourself. And if you ask, "Was I worth all of this?" I will answer you straightaway, "Yes, you were." Oh, I love you. I am not intending to abandon you. I am not driving you out into some salt flat and telling you, "Make camp here and dig in." That was someone else.

I'm saying, "Go to a safe place and be safe and do these things if you choose, for there are greater things coming." I will be with you through all of this. I will be with you, with your thoughts, after you finish reading these words. And I will be with you in the greatest thought of all — in your slumber, where I will show you and help you see things about yourself, tonight, and other nights when you slumber. And they're not terrible things; they are grand things.

Now when you pick this book up again, we will address some very interesting earthy truth. Some of it you have read before; some of it you have never seen in print. And I dare say that from the information to come you will have quite a few realizations.

Now, may I suggest that you stop reading now and take some nourishment and rest yourself at this point in assimilation. And may I further suggest that you do it in great joy as you contemplate what new information you have acquired. Put it in your personal storage system, in your mind, but mostly put it in your heart and allow yourself to feel. If you are angry, ask yourself why. If you are afraid, ask yourself why you are choosing fear. And if your ideas start to bubble to the surface, embrace them; we will manifest those ideas together and bring them into manifested destiny. Bargain?

PART II

The Waltz Continues

FOR THOSE OF YOU who rested before proceeding to this point, let me explain what may have happened for you in the sleep state. There are many of you who were asked, in your slumber, to take a deeper look at what you were dreaming. And there are some who were asked to look through the window and to see things, and the visions that played before your eyes are important things in your life that are coming forward. And yet you may not remember them. And that is all right, for looking ahead and seeing is often accompanied by some emotion. And if the emotion is strong, it's likely to be forgotten when you awaken, but it is there, right under the surface. Just scratch the surface with recognition and it will come back to you.

The Lazy Approach to Victimization

The elements of your socioeconomic system displayed here are extraordinarily accurate, and it is with dismay that I tell you I know there is an "accepted resolve" in many of you. Many of you are willing to simply accept what "real" life gives you. And that, dear readers, is very much a lazy approach to victimization.

You know, there are individuals in this country of yours who are always willing to shoulder the burdens placed upon them and who don't question why they are so burdened. Indeed, there are such individuals, of course, all around the world, but most pertinent to you are those in your country. And you have a lot of them. They don't ask, "Why am I in this position?" They don't ask,

"Why should I allow this to be my situation?" "Why should I be imprisoned and enchained to support a system that does not work for my greater good?" They don't ask. Why? Because they don't want to know; because if they knew, they are afraid they would have to stand up and say, "No."

Divine human beings, think about this for a moment. Certainly that which is termed God, the IS, is not provable to monkey mind. And it's not unprovable either. All of this is rolling out in the great mind of God, and your mind is the distinctive divine replica of the mind of God, the Eternal Mind, the IS, the All In All, the Forever And Ever And Ever — you are the same, it all comes from the same source.

Genius Is Not the Known; It Is the Unknown Realized

Your physical body is capable of brilliant things. Your brain, as well, is capable of receiving greater knowledge, greater thought-frequencies, genius. Yes, genius! Genius is not the known; it is the unknown realized. And genius, for each of you, lies in bringing forward the opening of the greater mind. You only use one-third of what you have now.

Your Life Is a Manifestation of Your Attitude

Now, let's go back and take a look at the divinity of the human being. If you are emulating in willed choice a replica of God Almighty, that is, if you are acting like you know you are God Man-ifest, then you have the instruments available to you. And the grandest instrument of all is the capacity to receive thought and to emotionally embrace that thought into creativity, into form. For destiny is just thoughts that have been emotionally embraced. Collectively, they are called your attitude. And that's how your life is. Your life is a manifestation of your attitude!

And yet, here are these human beings who have been hypno-tized into lethargy. They have accepted technology made afford-able, made lazy. Here is the divine human being who can no longer think for himself, who has relinquished what is the human being's inalienable right. The divine right to think and to choose is what makes you different! That is why you are divine! You possess the capacity to embrace unlimited thought and make it applicable. You can make it happen!

You are God's divine purpose. You are flesh and blood, completely loved without judgment, and in complete grace you are allowed your image — the flesh-and-blood creation of yourself so that you may explore your greater self; that is all there is. And you are allowed to demonstate all that you are, not just in a thinking process, but in a living process. What good is it just to think it when you can live it? If it isn't lived, it's nothing. It doesn't exist; it is only thought without form. And when I look upon social consciousness in the human drama, I see entities who have capable minds, who have capable bodies, and they are like leeches. They are living off of others. And they are capable, through desire, of being individuals. And I see them expecting the whole of the world to take care of them because they seem incapable.

I see those who take care of these people rendering that care in charity and love. That is a virtue *forever,* yes. But if you are the one who is living off of the fruits of someone else's hardened labor, when you are capable of genius — you have fallen into yet a greater stupor. You have refused life and yet, by your very existence, you must be provided for and taken care of.

Democracy Gives Birth to Tyrants

I see what has been called the middle class of this country. Did you know that without the middle class you could have no republic? A democracy gives birth to tyrants. A Republic is a sovereignty of the people. I see your middle class supporting the idealism of what you call a democracy. I see your middle class supporting the rich and supporting the poor. And I see your middle class, through shouldering their burdens, accepting everything your government is handing down to them.

There Will Be Outrage in This Country

There will be outrage in this country when your tax structure is raised. Yes, there will be! There are still some outrageous individuals who are individual enough to realize they shouldn't be burdened for the sake of the rich becoming richer through their investments. And there are still some outrageous individuals who see through political movements that would insist that you take care of the mobs in the streets who have chosen to retire from the existence of life; some see through the political cleverness in this ruse.

And some of you will see through this enslavement to a debt, yes! People think that the government prints the money. It does not! You are supporting a debt incurred through manipulation of good intent and you are continuing to pay something to someone who is not even part of this country. The attitude of the middle class supports this, and as a result you are the salvation of a democracy that honors the rich and supports the mobs. The middle class represents the absolute equality of a republic. But in your democracy, they are the animals of burden and you accept it! Because you have also accepted your own ignorance. You have resigned yourself to never discover what your rights always were! You have resigned yourselves to the belief that this is the price you pay for freedom. It is not! It is the price you pay for enslavement.

So I look upon you, God's glory, and I see you recoil from your own capacity to embrace the liberty of thought and the momentum of emotion, because your society has become so set and so accepting of regulation that if you are a thinker then your face becomes recognizable. And there is a great tendency for those around you to ostracize you and, indeed, even slander you. There is a price to pay in becoming yourself, but it is the only way to freedom.

So I observe God, flesh and blood, unrealized. And it is easy from that vantage point to see how the mountebanks, carpetbaggers, rascals, indeed how the Graymen could presume an initial goal of ruling the world through the monetary system, and in the process break the back of the middle class, a fervent goal of theirs. Because as long as there is a middle class your democracy and the republic still stand.

Stay with me here; this is important. Elitism is threatened by your very existence, and it is threatened by the power you could wield, and it is tremendously threatened by the possibility of your enlightenment. And I am not necessarily speaking of what is taught in the system called schooling. I am speaking of a historical enlightenment, and the works to support this information are readily available in many places, to help you understand what really happened. So that you no longer have to settle for what you were told happened.

Your Country Is Really Only an Illusion

Your government has failed you. Your country is really only an illusion whose reality is kept alive by your Constitution and your Bill of Rights. That is your only protection against a wholly enslaved society that is given entertainment, given beer — what was called mead in my time — given wine, and it is given its pay. All of your small comfort zones are readily available; the Graymen have seen to this. And so you are lulled, and you think this is what living freely is all about.

Your government is really owned by the money people, the international bankers. Your last great King, the last President, endeavored to create America's own great bank, which would have set up the system for the government to print its own money backed by its own value of gold. And your country could have done this. But instead you have people in the markets screaming that they are losing their investments because the government isn't playing the game. This is a betrayal and a conspiracy of greed levied against the middle class.

This is not to say that, from border to border, you don't have a land you can call your own, because at the present moment if you own land you can still call it yours. And this is not to say that the structure of a democratic republic is not intact — it is. But when the one-world government and the idealism of the Graymen go

full-thrust forward, and the card is issued when the world monetary system collapses, your Constitution and your Bill of Rights
will be restructured to suit the New World Order. And the freedom you have today will fall into antiquity. That is the plan.
Which doesn't necessarily mean it will happen, but that is the plan.

There is more to life than watching a soapy opera on the "tele";
there is more to life than being hypnotized into ignorance by
entertainment. There is knowledge to be sought for your own
personal awareness. There is understanding that helps unlock the
doors of your own *personal* illumination and gratification. Peace
of mind comes from complete sovereignty. And part of sovereignty is knowing what is going on; so that as you look through
the window, you can assert yourself and your own family, and
you can place them out of harm's way.

Not all, but most of your country will accept the horrific
depression that is coming. Most of the already hard-pressed workers will accept the coming fate. And why is this coming? Who
says it's time for a depression? Who says it's time for inflation?
Who has the last word? Those who own the money do. And the
ultimatum has been given to your government.

Reagan was given an ultimatum and his naiveté was sorely
devastated. Only toward the end did he realize how little liberty
he had as President to take action. Only toward the end did he
realize the limits of his actual power. From the point of that realization foward, he simply attempted to avoid the inevitable; as a
result, he was ridiculed through the world. What happened to him
was intentional, I'll have you know. And you think the entity
seemed irresponsible. He was fighting with a terror inside of him.
He was fighting the consciousness of righteousness, because he
did not want to deceive the American people and yet he had the
pressure of all the world financiers on him. And he had the entire
American public on him, saying it was his fault for not doing
something about this terrible debt you are saddled with.

The ultimatum they have given your government is that no
more money is going to be printed and the economy, your ability

to make money, is going to be tightened. And the mammoth depression to follow is, in a sense, just another part of the game that is played out for the purpose of retribution. In other words, they are creating your depression to set the American people up for the next step in their greater world purpose.

When your Federal Reserve will not print money and your international banks will no longer lend you money, and when foreign investors no longer participate in your economy, you have a massive depression. And what brings a nation out of a depression? War, which is great for the economy, but not so wonderful for those who have to fight it. But it does provide jobs and has been said to inspire an economy. Or, runaway inflation might help. Or, a new economic system; hence the debit card.

Now, the term "runaway inflation" I do not fully understand. I'm hearing it, here and there, and what I am seeing is excess paper. Is that a proper definition? Yes! Either way, someone pulls the strings and gives the word. It's not something that just happens to you. Because of the lethargy of the American people and their intentional ignorance, this is something that comes and goes and you seem to think you have to go with the tide.

Now this shouldn't outrage you, and it needn't be something you're embarrassed not to know. It should be something you learn. Indeed, you should take a step further to investigate and learn for yourselves instead of watching soapy operas all day. You should read, understand, and become completely enlightened. And if you're blocked by a particular prejudice, that prejudice could be your ultimate, not just financial, downfall. It could, in fact, mean your survival.

So here you are, God's grand, immaculate people. You love, you are merciful, you are ongoing; and to you — who *have* choice and complete manifested destiny — you are setting up a further tyranny through ignorance *and* superstition. And I wish to talk about that.

Enlightenment Is About Life

ENLIGHTENMENT isn't about crystals and it isn't about channeling. It isn't about hokey-pokey things. It is about life. Because life *is* a divine principle. Enlightenment is about the human drama, about being a *divine* entity. And it is about having the courage to live the life experience in divine peace of mind, in free spirit, and in complete freedom. You were meant to have the capacity to explore greater concepts, to conceive of vast probabilities, and to range into the uncharted unknown itself. And why haven't you changed? Why haven't people evolved further? They have found a comfort zone, idealized by their altered ego, and played upon and supported by those who *understand* them and how to enslave them.

When do you think? Music blares at you continuously. The tele runs endlessly. And you talk endlessly. When do you have the opportunity to embrace something greater than petty entertainment? Silence is a yet-to-be-evoked power, and it is more powerful than the Greymen, indeed, more powerful than enslaving laws and dogmas. It is a power that bespeaks freedom, and freedom in a continuum. Do you know that you do not have a continuum if you do not have freedom? That is a great truth.

Here is the middle class — struggling, revolting, *accepting* what is coming. Here are the infinitely rich who despise this message, who despise any other action than that which they have programmed the middle class to take. After all, anything that brought you out of your lethargy could be a threat to their fortunes, don't you know?

In this awakening process, I ask that you listen to youself. And be mindful of what you feel, for what you feel is coming out of a clarified knowingness, albeit suppressed for a while. Brave and courageous entities will appear in the days that are coming, and I am speaking literally of days, not years. They are coming forward with a truth that is as I have spoken. It will be like what I have told you here; the story of what is really going on. And more and more people will have the opportunity to hear this knowledge from someone they can relate to, someone just like them. And it won't be called a cult then. And it won't be called dangerous — it will be called a truth. Their seeds are already growing, and they are the people of the people.

There Are a Lot of Christians and Not Many Christ-ians

It would take me no more than the rest of this day to name you the rare individuals in religious communities whose love of God was deeper than their love of artifacts, dogma, and practices, yet who represented the clergy, represented the ministry, represented all religions in the profound truth of goodness and eternal mercy; individuals who had divine respect for the human being and lived life in a truly Christ-like way. You know, there are a lot of Christians and there are very few Christ-ians that have labored and helped humanity, not simply because of their religion — that has nothing to do with it — but because of their innately divine and grand inner being and because they truly loved their brothers.

Such grand individuals are sprinkled throughout your history. And many of them would have gladly died for you, because what was death to them but merely a transfiguration? They had no fear of death and would have given their lives for any one of you. That is how great they were, for they were aligned with that which was within them, and they were truly moved by the Spirit, the Spirit we are speaking about here with regards to the Days a-coming. These great men were not controlled by their altered ego, their own prejudices, or even their own life. Spirit moved them.

The clergy, the religions should have felt so worthy to have had such grand people. There are a few still left this day. But religion has failed the people. The truth of God and the ultimate of Christ realized within, however, has not. The truth of God and the ultimate of Christ realized will never fail you.

I want you to know who the Catholics blamed for the Black Plague of the 14th century. The Catholics condemned the Jewish people. They said the "curse of the Jewish people" caused the Plague, and with that battle cry they enforced the destruction of a people. You've always got to have someone to blame something on, don't you? So, the Jews were imprisoned and murdered and their property was seized and their goods were confiscated, and it was all taken back to the conquering kingdom. And this action was supported by religion — yes, it was.

Do you know that this fundamentally great religion, Catholicism, has always depended upon the economic situation of the world? Know you that it has betrayed its people for eons? Not all, not all, but many. For they have kept their people in ignorance; they have continued to divide men against their women and women against their men. They have not allowed the equality of the human being. They separate people, they don't bring them together. Their practices are separating practices, not bringing-together-in-peace-and-love practices.

And even today you ostracize those who are burdened with a plague, because of the sexual preference choice they made in this life. This is an outrageous thing to do in the name of God! For we are all God, created of the essence of that Essence. And even now you would keep these people in darkness, encouraging hate and superstition.

Your Book of books has been altered, in its translation from the original scripts into Latin, to fortify and to support the dogma of the ruling church. The heads of religion have available to them an audience of millions. Why don't they speak and tell you what the beast really is? The beast is not a spirit liken unto me. It is the very enemy that supports them!

But they keep their faces turned away, they don't speak, because the airways would not be open to them if they spoke the truth. If they said unto their people, "These are the times that are a-coming. This is the prophecy. And by the spirit that moves within me, this is how it is understood. Yeshua ben Joseph is not coming through the air to rescue you before tribulation. There was never the mention of rapture in the Book of books — it was created." They will not say that. Instead, the only path to salvation is their word. And how do they keep that word held together? How do they "own" you? Through superstition; through demons and devils; through wicked people who will crucify you and say, "I did it *because I loved your soul.*"

So, they cloak the truth from millions of people. What is the continuing truth of God? Did it end 2,000 years ago, and how accurately was it recorded 200 years after the event? Or do you suppose that God possibly has the ability to go forward?

There are millions of people who hate and despise anyone who doesn't believe what they believe. And millions are superstitious of anything that is not within their clique and their religion. They are superstitious of free thinking. Because someone has to think for them, and someone has to live for them, and someone else has to tell them what to do. And so the messengers of the last days get the label boogieman, beast, Antichrist. And I know they have tried to label me in an effort to keep you from hearing the truth!

So ears are turned away and truth is never heard because people are steeped in fear and superstition. And they are expecting a real beast, vile and ugly with ten horns, to come out of the sea and devour people. That is how they see it! They see a devil coming from within the Earth chasing people around with a pitchfork, herding them into an eternal burning pit. And they are glad this demon exists because he is their messenger of retribution for those who will not listen to them: "If you don't listen to me, you are going to burn in hell." Right? Can you imagine?

And there are millions who don't suspect anything about what is coming. They don't suspect the real danger. They have no idea what the true prophecy is. And they are kept in their ignorance, intentionally diverted, so that they spend their time worrying about their own sins and iniquities. And if they don't have any sins, some will be made up for them to worry about. They are told whom to fear. They are told who is evil. Their attention is diverted to everyone else but themselves and they are kept in a crusading march of complete ignorance.

The major religions have betrayed their people, and some of their leaders know the truth. But they can't afford to say anything. Their ministry depends on keeping the fear out there. Their fortune depends on it, their power depends on it and their leadership depends on it. And, in a sense, they are no better than those who scream about the hole in the stratosphere while continuing to burn fossil fuel.

Personal need, personal truth, is attributed to the glory of God, to the kingdom of heaven found within you. And it's simply a matter of choice. It always has been. Either you can listen to a faint spirit, a truth, a voice, a knowingness, an emotional feeling that starts off faintly, or you can disregard it and look for someone whose opinions, truth and sentiments you can echo.

The survivors of what is coming will have the instincts of a bird in the changing season, the understanding of the wild animals who know where to go. Isn't that a compliment, to have such an instinct? It is the greatest thing that can be said about the beginning understanding of survival.

There are entities from various religious backgrounds who have been chosen, because they chose to listen to, and to react to, the God that surrounds them and moves with them. They have the fortitude and the courage to interpret the prophecies, and they are speaking a truth. They are working for enlightenment. And although what they are saying is still totally within their chosen belief, it is a divine interpretation that rings true with what you are reading here.

These grand people are not working against you — they are with you, they are part of the radical few of God coming to a greater end.

Within your government, blessed as it is with so many excreted politicians, will come a handful — and I am speaking of a human handful — who, through righteousness, and the bearing of the Lord God within their Being, will speak out.

So, from the religions the radical few are being chosen, and the government will supply a very few, and then, of course, you — if you so choose.

And so, you see, this book is very important. Because the truth must be spread among the middle class. Because they are the ones who need to hear it.

Inevitably the yoke of the tax burden will be placed on the back of the middle class. What will it take to wake them from their lethargy? Either a very strong runner, so you get the point without a doubt, or the fact that you'll wake up one day on the bottom when you were just on the top. Bless it, whatever it takes to waken you with the ability to understand. The truth will be there when you're ready for it.

And the more of you who hear the truth and recognize its ring, the more of humanity that will have a greater opportunity to survive everything you are up against in these manifested days of destiny. The man who laughs at this and says it doesn't exist is a fool. He is a fool and he will die a fool. And he only furthers his frivolity when he doesn't make the choice to find out the truth for himself. The fact is, some of these truths will only become important to you when you experience the harshness of their reality.

If all the Gods slumbering in the comfortable lethargy of the middle class woke up, they could create a republic because there are so many of them. Too great are the numbers to stop such a forward march. They could take the government back from the politicians and create a republic like Solon's Republic, where every educated, enlightened person helped to create a coexisting government, holding truth steadfast, with a constitution and an inalienable bill of rights that allowed every human being to prosper and to grow. Because the understanding is obvious: what you are affects the whole.

And if this great middle class woke up, there would never, ever, ever be a national debt, for their government of the people, the republic created by the people, would have the power to issue its own notes backed by its own commodities and its own resources. This country would sustain *forever* if its people were like the sweet earth, the very ground, for that ground would be divine and supportive. All people could live, without want and without debt. When you create interest, you create debt, and that would not be the basis for creating this new government. And it would truly be the first republic ever. Solon's *dream* of a republic was the ideal — it has never been manifested because of the lethargy and ignorance of the people.

Contrary to what you may see here at first glance, I am not a revolutionary. I bespeak the glory and the options latent within each individual on the face of this Earth. And it isn't that you don't know this, for deep down inside you know all of this. And it isn't that those who don't read this book don't know the truth at some level. It is that your great country needs to restore her virginity, and the people taking the power back from the usurpers would restore the purity of spirit. And we shall see if that happens or not.

The Prophets Are Already Amongst the People

The prophets have been chosen by their courage. They are not afraid of ostracism. They can speak, and they are already amongst the people. They are coming from every walk of life. And we shall see. We shall see if the people of this world, in particular of your country, for that is what we are addressing, are truly as ignorant, helpless and powerless as the Graymen are betting you are. So be it.

Back to the Basics

NOW, LET'S GET DOWN to personal needs. I know you've already heard the message in this book, but I need to address the procrastinators. You know who you are. You're excellent at talking about doing something to get prepared. You go to lunch at the chic spot and chat about preparing for the Days To Come. But you haven't done anything! How can I get your attention on this matter? How can I make you understand how imperative this is to your very survival? The greatest priority in your life, right now, should be storing food — number one. Store food! Food! Food! FOOD! FOOD!

Not only is storing food an assurance against a lousy economy, and an assurance against the reactions from it, but it is also an assurance that you will eat through the changes brought about in nature. Storing food is number one because you can have all the gold in the world, you can have all the clothing in the world — why, you can even have all the silver in the world and all the investments in the world, you can have all of your art pieces, all your diamonds, emeralds, rubies, and even a piece of canvas, "but ya ain't gonna be able to eat 'em." And sure as shooting, if that's where all your priorities are, you'll starve to death and someone will confiscate your art and your jewels and they'll take 'em off and make a bundle — more than likely the person who did put up the food!

Storing food — I know, I know. It's true, it's not a very glamorous thing to do. It's something you don't want to talk a lot about in public. You don't want to discuss canning jars and the shelf life of bulgur wheat with your social friends. But listen, without food all that I have taught you thus far will mean nothing. You won't be here! You have to be doers in this knowledge, not a leech who says "I know it all. I read the book," but then doesn't do anything; then you will succumb to some very painful days.

No matter which side of the bread you butter, it still comes down to food. All the way across the board, all your priorities should go into food — two years' worth for yourself and anyone you're responsible for. And listen, if you've stored two years' worth, don't you sit back and say "I've done it" while berries are still growing on the bushes outside your window and apples are falling on the ground and rotting. This isn't simply a checklist so that when you get precisely to two years' worth you can go out to play! Take advantage of your bounty, particularly when you live in an area that is bountiful. It may not always be that way.

Now, there is more about the food — don't stop reading now! Seeds. Put seeds in airtight containers and store them. Store every imaginable thing you ever conceived could be planted, even if it is not indigenous to the area you live in, because times are definitely a-changing. Are you with me? Think of things you haven't previously considered and store their seeds.

And every opportunity you get, purchase a tree; do so expeditiously. And plant a fruit-bearing tree every chance you get. Put them everywhere around you.

Now that's enough about food. The second thing you need to do to is to buy gold and silver coins or bullion, coins preferably. If you can't afford to purchase gold, then buy silver. They are tangibles. They are going to grow in worth. Buy them now, while you can.

Let's talk about property. Now, I am not speaking of condos in the city. The cities will be the most dangerous places to live in the Days To Come; even in these days they are not safe places.

Get out of the city. Purchase land close to small towns. Don't live so far into the hills that no one can find you there either. Buy land: land you can grow things on; land that will not only support you, but render barter in the Days To Come. Get it?

Now why would I tell you city dwellers to get out of your city? Because when the Earth changes come, water reserves will be poisoned — it only takes one great zipper bursting open to poison the groundwater; underground water mains will be damaged. And bursting zippers will break up nuclear plants. And then there's famine, a natural result of weather changes. Where would you grow food in the city? The cities are the most dangerous places to be. Move away from them.

More and more enlightened people will be moving to the country, far away from the main cities. Many will move as a result of reading this book and many more will move because they feel the pull inside. When you have acquired your land, you have taken the next precaution to sustain yourself. And you can never lose on land that is purchased; you never will. And you'll never lose on feeding yourself as economically as possible. And you'll never lose on gold and silver. So there is nothing you will be doing to destroy your fortune!

Now, let's look at how we can get you out of the city. If you live there now and your work is there now, then find a way to rent in the city and prepare to purchase land outside of the city, land that belongs to you. It can be called an investment. If you have a hovel in the city, it is my advice that you take an enormous loan against it, but make certain that you are protected in the language of the loan. Make sure it is the kind of loan that allows you to walk away from it in case of natural catastrophe, so they can't go after everything else you have; a nonrecourse loan. From loan instruments well placed on your hovel in the city, you can afford to purchase land in the country. Do it.

On to the next item. Look around you. It's easy to see what you need next. If you had no electricity, how would you survive? Purchase equipment, and tools, and those things you can work with elbow grease. Look at the electrical equipment you need to keep your body in shape, for example. You lean on belts that vibrate. You run on treadmills. Then you walk into the bathroom and plug in a cord and blow-dry your hair! Think about it! Instead of running on your treadmill, put it to use.

Masters: act as if there were no electricity and prepare all things so that you could live accordingly. Remember the inventor in a far-off land working with the light of the sun? Well, just hold on and become self-sufficient until he can bring his idea home to you. Bargain?

Buy everything you would need to "dig in" and hold you over. And what will you do when you have done all of those things? Well, you can puff up your chest and you can say, "Indeed, come what may, I am ready for it." Bully for you. Because there is nothing grander than peace of mind.

Do you know the price of being in debt and having to slave to support that debt? It is a terribly high price. The real price is not even in dollars; it is in stress, and worry, and anxiety. Get rid of your debts. You can choose to continue to be in debt, but for your personal sake you should alleviate the burden. Because being sovereign is having peace of mind. And what will it feel like to have created a sovereignty for yourself wherein you cannot lose, any way you look at it, and through that sovereignty to have provided a legacy for your family? Because it is not advisable to be in debt in the Days To Come, because then you will get the mark of the Beast whether you want it or not — the debit card.

Peace of mind — knowing you can slumber at night, knowing that you are prepared. Fear, anxiety and stress come from knowing you are not prepared. And if it demands that you carve down your enormous appetite, do so. And when I speak of appetite, I do not mean what you eat. I am speaking of all those things you think you cannot do without at present. Delineate the difference between personal need and personal desire. The difference may be survival.

And when you have done all these things and you still have excess paper money, buy more land — land! Do not put it back into your banking system; purchase land. And if you have enough gold and silver to last you until 2042, purchase land, but not in the city. Instead, buy land in places where things can grow upon it.

And if you still have more paper left, help your brethren to help themselves. Because there are many of you who are very fortunate in your genius and there are many of you who are struggling for that genius. Many of you are doers, and are worthy of help; and some of you don't do anything, and are not worthy of help.

You see, if you accomplish storing all your food, buying your land, getting your equipment, and helping where you can, you can withstand everything, from nature to the Graymen. You won't have to take the debit card. You can refuse it. You won't need it to pay off your debt or support your family. Don't you understand? That is the reason they want you in debt. But you can decline it and say, "No, I will not take it. For I do not need to generate capital or to buy and sell. I am self-sufficient."

And those of you who are in transition, endeavoring to fulfill all of these things, you are not without help. And though you don't have many things, there are provisions that are coming, and food is coming for you. There is a force that will help you, but you must unlock your own awareness and become a doer. Not because you are scared to death but because that is the emotion within you. And because that is what you are aligned with. You will not go unheard or unhelped, I assure you.

And those of you who have families who do not see any of this as a truth, you are in a very precarious position and you are putting your family there along with you — yes, you are. The greatest thing you can do is to save up your food and apply your savings to these investments as best you can. There are going to be enough things happening very shortly that will cause the people either to revolt or to start making dynamic changes in their lives.

And if it is simply a matter of relationships and you are going forward and living the Lord God of Your Being and someone is holding you back, leave that person! Go forward — go forward.

Banks! Remember I told you that many of your banks already have your debit card? Ask them if they do. And if they do, it would be wise and prudent of you to only use it if you have nothing else as a vehicle for transferring money — paper money. Do *not* purchase your gold from banks, for they have a record of you.

If you do all of these things, you shall survive all of the days to come. And you will survive with dignity, with liberty, and, indeed, with freedom. And you will do it without compromising your intelligence. And you will do it without compromising or giving away or prostituting your truth. You will simply have regained what you lost in the industrial revolution. And that is *sovereignty,* absolutely it is!

Superconsciousness Never Comes When You're Chasing Your Tail

When you regain the full understanding of freedom of choice, you move back into evolution. You will be progressive human beings, divinely endowed, manifesting a destiny that offers Superconsciousness. But superconsciousness never comes to one who is running around chasing his tail over the same old problem. You can never have a grand and exalted stroke of pure genius if your whole body of thought and emotion is tied up in the worry of stress and strain and indebtedness.

You can never glimpse profound vision if your whole attitude is surrounded by what you lack. You can never see what is sitting in the sky if your head is down and you're busy fingering your worry beads over a broken love affair. And you will never see the glory in what is coming if you are in front of your tele absorbed in some illusionary problem. You understand what I am saying. I know you do.

How are you going to see your great brothers? And they are coming; some are already here. And they know you. How are you going to see them if you never look up? And how will you hear the phone ring above all of the music blasting in your ears? How will you know that that great tone is them trying to reach you? You know those tones ringing in your ear that many of you hear, and many more will hear? It is your great brothers saying, "I'm tuning in. Are you there?" How will you hear them if you are so busy doing something else? Because the great tone many of you

will hear is not from impaired hearing. Don't let anyone tell you
it is.

I cannot make you do any of these things. And I wouldn't want
to. But I would desire that you, through your own will, find the
truth and act on it. Know that I am in your corner, because you are
my brother and my sister. And you are. But only you can enact
your great will. And I as your equal brother cannot tell you what
to do, and, certainly, I cannot make you do it. That is a game for
someone else, not one that I will perpetuate.

There is so much knowledge in this book that you could go
straightaway and manifest the wheels into gear. There is enough
knowledge here to show you not to be afraid of anything. And if
you are lacking courage, perhaps that is your only fear. And that is
by choice, too. There is nothing you can't do, but everything you
can do. It is just by choice that you draw the line, where you put
the limits.

And When the Government Has Starved Out All the Farmers and They End Up Owning the Land, They Will Own a Dust Bowl

And there are some of you who will read this but won't lift a
finger to do anything because you don't think any of this will
really come true. Oh, you think this is a great story, but that's as
far as it goes. Your time is running out. Your economy is erratic
now. And one day the marketers will scream they made a fortune
and the next day they will have lost twice as much. And what will
start out as a relief through inflation will turn out to be the
severest depression the people have ever known. And when the
government has starved out all of the farmers and sent them into
that miserably dehumanizing state called bankruptcy and they
end up owning the land, they will own a dust bowl.

Your time is running out, but that must be by choice as well.
Now, if you've been driven crazy by what you've read here and
you have an emotional breakdown because of what you've read,

that's your choice. It will not be because you're not loved. You are loved more dearly than you can imagine. It is simply a matter of choices. That's what I've been talking about. And if you say your monetary means are limited, then ask the Lord God of Your Being to manifest other ways and means for you and it will happen. All you have to do is ask.

And if you settle for your rut in life, it is because you never learned to look at your mistakes as learning experiences rather than mistakes. Because as long as you call anything in your life a mistake, you will draw the experience to you continuously, over and over and over, until you look at it and say, "What did I learn here?" Only when you own what you learn will you be free of it. And when you own it, it will give you up.

So. If you are in the doldrums of self-pity and you choose to call this "programming," then how many times have you repeated the same pattern? And what is it you need to learn? That self-pity doesn't bring any rewards — it only brings death. But dignity and self-respect renew and regenerate the option called life.

Ask Your Plant, "May I Have This Tomato?"

It's true, you've been spoiled. Do you know that word, spoiled? Smelly. Because you think you have had it so good and so easy. Learn to be the doers again. How grand it is to take a piece of earth and turn it under and feel the moisture slip through your fingers as you bless the land. And you sprinkle it with holy water and bless your seeds and put them in. And you watch the little darlings bloom! How grand a feeling that is! And to ask your plant, "May I have this tomato?" You don't take from a plant, you ask it! And the more you ask, the happier it is to please. When you have planted that way and loved the land, that is a grand feeling. And it is as empowering as it is satisfying.

And if you are living in the city and you just can't see your way to do any of the rest of this, at least go find a place where you can put up a garden and go tender it. And bring the foodstuffs back and store it. At least begin somewhere. It brings dignity, not self-pity. It is a start at doing.

And There Is Really Nothing More Splendid than a Woman Who Realizes She Doesn't Have to Depend on a Man

And there is really nothing more splendid than a woman who realizes that she doesn't have to depend on a man. There is nothing more splendid in all the universe than a woman who discovers that it is not through a man that she finds salvation.

That statement was not intended to degrade the men, don't you know, but rather to encourage all of you to say, to whatever is holding you back, "This is no longer my excuse, I am my own individual. I shall do this thing." So be it.

The Radical Few of God

PERSONAL SURVIVAL and the radical few of God. Well, that truth is written in time — it is the inevitable manifested destiny. And glory to those of you who have read and contemplated and gained and earned this knowledge. Splendid times are coming in Superconsciousness as soon as the dance is done. And the ghostly Gray dancers are getting more frantic, for the tempo has accelerated; their movements are getting more rapid by the day. Know that with their push to hurry up and succeed in reaching their goal, they are also pushing Superconsciousness. Because Superconsciousness and the Glory of God and the appearance of the Host comes when the vacuum collapses. And the vacuum is choice.

When there is no longer a choice; when it is simply the way it is for the whole of the world, for governments and kings, and monarchs and aristocrats; when your ability to choose collapses — and that is the aim of One World Order — then that is the end of time. For time has always been relative to man and his purpose. And it is also the end of the Age of Tyrants that has been supported by the altered ego. The altered ego is anti-God. It always has been.

And listen, there isn't any one of you reading this book or anyone anywhere in the population that could ever stop the onslaught of nature and her healing. Not even a whole nation of people could stop her movement. If nature has to step in and intervene, the zippers where many of the great beasts, computers, sit will be torn asunder. And weather patterns are shifting dramatically.

125

And what of those great volcanos, one in Europa and one on an island, and one more, by the way, that is brewing in Russia? If they come to life, it would have the effect of creating winter in summer. Either way nature takes action, the Graymen will be destitute in their ultimate plan and nature will have won.

And yes, there will be many people that would perish in any of these situations. There always have been when nature takes that route. There was a great and glorious time in a place called Pompeii. Pompeii was where the aristocrats lived. They took their summer vacations there — you call them vacations, I call them holidays — irrespective of what they were living beside. It didn't really make any difference to them, because their vacations were more important than the possiblity of this brewing tiger about to escape her cage. It was alive and smoking and rumbling for the longest time. Do you think that stopped their sojourns to vacation at the "right" spot? It didn't. So, why should it be such a terrible thing that so many perished in the eruption at Pompeii? It was not as if they didn't know. They knew.

So, it is by choice; it always has been. And there are very few of you in this country who are not aware of where you live — or of what you are living on, to be precise. There are not very many of you who don't realize that changes are afoot. And violent natural changes will always affect feeble, screaming, crying, unfortunate mankind. But he has not been betrayed by nature, but by his own arrogance. He has been betrayed by his own altered ego and his image refusing to change.

So, nature will take violent actions and it will move to destroy the possibility of the Graymen's goal to create One World Government.

I can tell you something: when the food supply gets short and the people revolt, all those people who have held their tongues for so long are going to start screaming, and they are going to tell it all. And they will point fingers, and the truth will be let out to the whole world. And even in that, Superconsciousness will come. And if the plan of the Graymen succeeds and the vacuum collapses, you will see an Armada like you only thought existed in fairy tales. They do exist.

Imagine a world without an altered ego? Because when the altered ego is absorbed by the God within, that which sleeps densely in the image will begin to wake up, and you will begin to move into evolution in a forward thrust. Why can't you live longer here? Why can't you stop the aging process? And why can't you cure your diseases? Because all of these things are products of the altered ego, a collective attitude.

What you think, you are. Now, listen for a moment. I have watched you try to change the thought, which is the higher, by evoking the lower. In other words, I have watched you sit and stress and struggle and sweat and think until you turn purple. And you go nowhere. You are trying to travel into the unknown, far beyond your body, far into what you call another dimension. I have watched you try to move the body through a higher frequency rather than reversing that process. And when you sit and sweat and go nowhere, you create a fantasy to save face!

You Cannot Change the Thought from Mass; You Must Change the Thought

I have seen you endeavor to cure the body beginning with the mass rather than through that which created it and controls it — the attitude. I have watched you endeavor to solve an attitude problem by deliberately doing something to the flesh rather than to the attitude. You cannot change the thought from mass. It must change from the thought. Only then is mass altered, changed, accelerated.

Whatever the precise manifested destiny turns out to be here, whichever phenomenon acts first, it will be based on your collective attitude; that is what will create your tomorrow. Your personal reality is all centered in the nucleus called choice. And what will you choose? Will you choose self-pity? Will you choose pain? Will you choose rejection? Will you choose victimization rather than mastership? Everything you think you are, you are! And everything you are is the manifested destiny which the mass flows through. It is called life. And in this life, you are going to bring to yourself the opportunities that are afforded by that attitude, that nucleus, that control center.

Cosmic Glue and the Atom

Everything is coagulated thought. Every object is a thoughtful design created. Where do you think gross matter comes from — space? Where do you think life emerges from? What gives the cosmic glue to the atom? What is it that holds gross matter together; why do those little cells stay together? The thought that created it — it is held by the thought; that is why it has substance in mass.

Consider manifested destiny. You will not change your destiny by changing your body. You must change your destiny through the attitude in which you perceive your reality. You cannot go to the moon in this flesh and blood; only spirit can enter the unknown. So how do you drag along this excess baggage? By ceasing to become enlightened through the body but instead to become enlightened through the spirit — the self, the knowingness — through the unlimited process called God.

You Are What You Think You Are.
You Have Always Suspected It.

Listen, you: the more you know, the more knowledge you gain. And the more awareness you have, the greater the brain is pressed to open through the pituitary. Why does that little mass stay closed? Why is your brain only running on one-third power? Where is the other two-thirds? Where is the genius? Your life is emotionally made up of what you emotionally express. And your prosperity has only manifested in your destiny according to how you perceive your intelligence. And intelligence isn't based on schooling; it is based on the desire to know. Innate common sense is one of the grandest gifts you have — a hunger. The hunger to know. And the desire is there. It is coming through the center of your reality; it is the desire to know that you are what you think you are. You have always suspected it. I am only comfirming your own suspicions.

You Don't Get to the Great Thought Through Density

In Superconsciousness, which is coming, there is an availed reality which understands that in the focus of your life, you control it all. In Superconsciousness you will understand that spirit is not changed because of mass; mass is transformed according to the choice of attitude. That is why doing all the things that I see you struggle with won't change anything. You can wear all the crystal baubles you want. You can peer endlessly into crystal balls. You can drink a thousand cups of special herbal tea. And you can eat all the tofu in the world. And it won't change the spirit, the ego. It is a game. You don't get to the great thought through density; you create density through the great thought.

You will not take your body and ascend with it just because it is the fashion. In fact, if ascension is your aim you will surely die. Because wanting to ascend is the desire for death, and that is working through the mass, not the spirit. In the spirit there is eternal life. And there is only eternal life for the physical body when one realizes what creates life — you!

What do you think is meant by the statement, "The kingdom of heaven is within you"? What do you think it means? It means that it is by the grace of God within that all things are made possible unto you. Yes! And you have the capacity within your body to allow them to occur. You have the capacity to allow a great realization to manifest, and it waits. It has waited for you for centuries.

You could live a thousand years in great joy. You could have longevity and the grand concept of Superconsciousness, without an altered ego. As it sits there holding your spirit right at this moment, your body is wired, if you will, with the capacity to raise its physical vibration, to move into another realm through vibratory change. It can be commanded by the spirit, the I Am, the ego called God.

Superconsciousness Is Not What You Eat

Superconsciousness. It's not what you eat. It's not what you wear. It is what you *are*. And when the altered ego is intact and ruling the roost, it is the jailer, the guardian that keeps the God within from this natural expansion. It is the jailer — and it feeds on appearance, and it feeds on image. And it must have its own image reflected around it, to support it. The altered ego *inhibits* the God within from expression; that is why it is called the Antichrist.

The altered ego is also what keeps knowledge from entering the soul to be evolved upon. Why can't you remember anything you read? Because your altered ego doesn't want you to remember it, that's why. This waltz of the Graymen represents the idealism of the altered ego. And when their hour is finished, so that consciousness will end. And that is when Superconsciousness will come. Why is it called Superconsciousness? Why is it called the Kingdom of Heaven made manifest? Because when you absolve the altered ego as a learning experience, not a mistake, then the whole realm of your physical body comes alive. Alive! And the way you absolve the altered ego is through the God within, the power that works within you that allows you. When you embrace it and love it, learn from it and let it go, then you can really live.

The brain then begins to open because there are new thoughts pressing. What else is there to think about when you are no longer worrying about competing with someone else, undermining someone else, judging someone else, having malice and intolerance toward someone else? What is there left? You can contemplate and become the unknown, the world. You can express joy and love. And you can live in peace that passeth all understanding. Because the altered ego keeps malice, insecurity, unworthiness, and fear up front in your mind. When that is gone the brain opens up and the ego, the God within, yes, the Lord God of Your Being, comes alive in a great vitality. And that essence, that nucleus of your universe owns the whole of that universe, and it *grows,* your life grows, your awareness grows, your brain opens up. You encounter and embrace a grander thought, grander knowledge, the process of adventure called *unlimited.*

The Moment the Seventh Seal Opens, the Death Hormone Will Be No More

And the moment that the great seventh seal opens the pituitary, the death hormone will be no more in the body. The death hormone is in everyone's body at this time. It has been there since women began having their season of blood and men began to spill their seed. You got old as soon as that happened. There is a death hormone secreted from the pituitary and it is responsible for the shrinking of the thymus, which is centered near the heart cavity. This thymus is the longevity organ in the body. It is also the fourth seal. When you are a child, it is as large as a pear. When you are an adult, it is as small as a pea.

And right now, the thymus is shrinking continually. As it shrinks, the body shrivels. And as it shrinks the body is susceptible to disease. And finally, when it is virtually invisible, the body becomes broken down physically. And it is attitude alone that causes this in the body. It is your willing acceptance of attitudes that create your whole destiny, your reality, your environment.

When the altered-ego attitude is no longer in control and this seventh seal opens and the death hormone is removed, there is another hormone that is secreted into the body that activates the thymus. And it is through this great seal's growth that the buttons of cellular mass are pushed which allow for continuous and instant rejuvenation, over and over and over.

And why would you want to live so long? Because you have never lived, that's why. You've been stuck.

Superconsciousness is the sovereignty of the people of a free and original republic. It is a great experiment that will succeed. Because all the doors that have been shut to you will open. In Superconsciousness you will leave behind the tyranny and absolute stench of the human experience that you have lived, over and over and over again. You will leave behind the misery and the death and dying. You will leave behind the unhappiness and the enslavement to yesterday. You will join the forward thrust of evolution and go into a new time with a body fully capable of experiencing what is to be experienced.

Do you know why you can't see the light that surrounds your body, your great spirit — your aura, as you call it? Because your reality doesn't allow you to see it. Do you know why you can't see the energy that fills the room you are sitting in, that hangs off your light fixtures? Because the whole focus of your attitude has been in your little intimate world that has been guarded by the altered ago. And you will never see what you do not have the knowledge to see.

Don't you understand? You have to experience it; then the vision will be there, then you will be able to see. Why do some not see with the same sort of eyes that others see with? It is because their realities are different. Oh, they can talk a good game, but if they don't live it, they don't see it. Your eyes will naturally see what you have never seen before. For there is nothing I would love more than for you to see the light that is unseen; to despoil fear and superstition; to be able to see the glory of your own light, because you have never allowed yourself to see even that. In Superconsciousness you will have the eyes to see the host and the dimensions. And you will have the knowingness of the great kingdom that is coming: not only the exploration of the possibilities of your universe, but mansions unforetold and unimaginable. This is your heritage. It is the heritage of the human drama. And yes, there have been other humanoids in the mind of God. But I want you to know that not everyone made it big time. And for the most part their civilizations collapsed into decadence through this same vacuum process. In your civilization, however, you have great truth coming your way, and grand opportunity. And the meek will inherit the Earth and see the glory of God, for they will have the eyes to see it. And this civilization will not collapse. Know the truth. Be enlightened. Be engaged. Be knowing. Superconsciousness: the dreamed of, yet unexperienced, yet fully exponential possibility of the time at hand. It is worth hanging around to see for yourself. So be it!

You Are Never Truly Alone

W E ARE NEARING the close of what I have to say to you regarding the now. Know that this experience, this learning, has meant more than the time it has taken you to read these words. It has meant more than the gold you spent in buying this tome, and it has meant far more than the reasons you had for reading it. Look at yourself. Think how many people will read this message. Consider what you all have in common with one another. You are never truly alone. In all things that you endeavor, there are brothers and sisters abounding in all directions. But it is in aloneness that you make decisions such as where you go and what you read, as everything is your choice.

Never Regret a Choice

Never regret a choice! Because what you have chosen to do allows you to evolve; it's a divine declaration. And what may leave you with regret is really only part of further evolution. You never lose anything. It will come back — it will bloom again.

It fills my being with joy that you have read my words and your light will grow from it. I know the courage it has taken for you to sit there and address what is in front of you with a maturity of spirit, in love; not in fear. You are no weaklings, no spineless creatures of the unknown. You truly represent your heritage quite well. I'm very pleased. And one day you will be able to see just how happy I am; for you will see me in all my joy. And I will be very pleased at that.

Many of you have been through the fire, just to finish reading this book. I know. I know your denials, and your curses, and your rejections, and your excuses, and your wanderings, and all of that. But I had a great amount of knowingness and trust in your ability long ago, or I wouldn't be here. For I certainly have the ability to go someplace else and do other great things besides sifting through centuries of language to find the words that you will understand. It is most arduous work!

In all of your adventures since our meeting, you have gained greatly. Never deny the ground you've covered since you have known of me. For in the end, this will be the most rapid march you have ever undertaken. This will be your most progressive growth in the shortest time. And in the end you will say, "I would not have missed it for the world."

How Can You Prove the Immortality of a Thought?

No one has ever been able to put the Ram in a box. And for all that I have been on this plane, for all the things that I am accused of and responsible for, I allow. From density, it is impossible to understand a higher form. But when you understand the form from spirit, you are one with it. Density, and its image, the altered ego, would never understand the likes of me, any more than many of your peers can understand your journeying. They can't fathom it. How can you prove spirit in mass? What created out of mass could possibly capture spirit? How can you prove the immortality of a thought, of joy you can hear all the way into forever?

And why are so many people hostile to this understanding and this truth? And why are there so many imitators? Because they don't own the truth that is within them. It is one thing for someone to say you are part of the occult; it is another to laugh with them for saying it. Because it is a sign of personal dignity and freedom to have the sovereignty to make your own decisions — to have the wisdom to gain the options and knowledge that allow you to address the issues that are pertinent to your own destiny. If that is bizarre, the whole world needs to be bizarre!

Own what you own. Choose what is needed for you in your evolution. The truth is, in the time you've taken to read this book and contemplate this information, I have attempted to teach you many things, many repetitious things. And I have come at you from all angles, hoping to get a flicker of movement from you. And it is true, I have sent runners to some people that seem to devastate them, while other runners seem to bring them glory in the midst of misery. But it is all purposeful.

Listen, masters. What really is the greatness of a man's wealth if, in fact, it is his enslaver? And what is the piety of a woman's poverty if it is her enslaver?

The more you know, the greater your options. It has been a grand thing to help you broaden your options by giving you this information. You invested of yourself to acquire it. And I addressed you and laid it out there, because you deserve to know. I could have ignored the issues. I could have swept them under the carpet and simply reiterated meaningless words. But that would not have offered you the right to personal dignity through greater understanding. That is a truth.

I Came on My Father's Business, on a Beam of Love

There is no one else like me, because I am not owned on this plane. And it is not necessary for me to be popular, or to be accepted. Nor is it necessary for me to have kind words spoken on my behalf. And I have not prostituted the values or avoided the issues. I came here on my Father's business, on a beam of love. For I desired to do this. I did not come here to create a following but to cull individuals out of the herd of ignorance. Individuals who would, through the efforts of their own understanding and the courage to live their light, not only make a difference to their own life, but to the whole of the world.

It only takes one truly magnificent human being to give hope to so many. And there have been a few who have risen to the top of the mountain, to a place where their voice could be heard reverberating throughout the whole of the world, indeed, until it ricocheted off the stars. Individuals who, by the very virtue of rising to that pinnacle of fame, wealth, and respectability, have an opportunity to change the lives of millions of people. Because all the millions needed was a glimmer of light from a blazing entity, to show them it was possible for everyone to be that way. That's what hope is — an image, a light, truth, a reflection, something somewhere to help you begin the journey out of bondage. For you have certainly been in bondage.

Impeccability Doesn't Start in the Dictionary

Oftentimes the top is a place of revelry and power and abuse and misuse; and it becomes enslaving. Rare are the individuals who glimmer, through and through. Where does impeccability start? In the dictionary? That is only a philosophical definition; it is not truly a reality. Impeccability starts with an impeccable person. Love starts with those who have given respect to themselves, love to themselves, and have engendered this wonderful, beautiful jewel called the human being — which is the apple of the eye of God — with love rather than abuse. And through that love, they exemplify impeccability everywhere.

Your love is like the great central sun, for things grow in its warmth and you become a light. And where does the battle end and tolerance begin? When you have tolerance with yourself. When you hold yourself in dignity, from your own point of view. When you have tolerance for your capacity and for what seems like human error. If you have understanding, the grace of that understanding, tolerance and dignity emanates to everyone. Rare is the entity who is free of the chains of the world, who lives in a state of freedom, and has the capacity for tolerance of others. You can never tolerate anyone as long as you are owned by them. You can't tolerate your neighbors until you have resolved your own conflicts. You can't tolerate your family until you have understood that they are human beings, just like you.

Where Adventure Is Multifaceted and You Can Sleep under a Blue Moon, Unharmed

This business, this teaching, this love, this endowment was given so that by applying what you've learned, you can make choices that allow you to become that most immaculate human being. And there is not one of you reading this who does not have that capacity, if you choose to. Then you would live on to experience a kingdom that is worthwhile; where adventure is multifaceted and you can sleep under a blue moon, unharmed. These words were not meant to enslave you but to enhance the probabilities of you becoming who you really are; to enhance your human potential for joy, freedom, and God's love felt within. These words were not meant for turning one person against another, but for revealing ignorance and removing its veil through choice.

The New Age Is an Inside Story

The New Age, as this time has been called, never, ever, comes outside of a person. Change will. But the New Age never exists outside — it has to happen inside. It is an individual transfiguration of the human spirit releasing the past forever, with no regret, and owning the present with the full vitality of the courage to live happily and to sustain life. Like all things that become fashionable, fashion fades, but the light will live on; for it rings with truth, the power to do, and the understanding of life that makes the difference within a human being. It will live on forever.

It certainly did not gratify me to address you concerning all of the arduous things that are putting your environment in peril. And yet, I respect you. And I know full well that in the Lord God of Your Being you have the courage to see the truth in this, and to address it, and hear it, and through its emotional impact to begin to make the changes in your life that are so important to sustain life. I did not address you as anything other than the great Gods that you are. I have told you nothing that you cannot do. I have told you nothing that would waste or despoil anything. I have told you nothing that would put you in danger, but rather out of it. And I have told you not to despise the Earth, but to love it and all the changes that are more in number than you could possibly read about.

In broadening your knowledge by giving you this infomation, I am allowing you to know, "What's up, Doc." I like that phrase. Giving you information that allows you to make decisions is all I ever could have done in all these years in this outrageous form, with this limited body capacity. I have used all these words and visions, and runners, and given you many experiences to get you to here.

But those were only instruments, vehicles to get you where you are, called upon to help you engage. This is the end result; it always was: that Behold God will become a profound realism rather than a myth, a philosophy, a spiritual truth, so that you may live it. I know what your potential is — unfolding. I know what is locked up inside, and I know it has stayed locked up by choice as well. It is all a matter of what you want to do. And it is very relative to your life, as it always has been.

But ignorance is inexcusable. For either you choose to remain ignorant or you simply are because you have not had the opportunity to learn. Now you have the knowledge and you can no longer beg ignorance. And if you choose to put this book down and go back to the hustle and bustle and the "busyness" of violent people who smile at you with deadly eyes, then, by all means, return to your place where that is the norm. And if you go back to all of that and become engulfed, you will still have this knowledge. You will simply have set yourself up for victimization.

The Doers Are Going to Be the Seers

Remember the two great runners that are coming? It is remarkable, but actually seeing a phenomenon for yourself really changes your life. But oddly enough, in this circumstance the doers are going to be the seers, for they deserve what they will see. They will have earned it. That is what this is all about: earning the right to an expansive awareness. And even those who dismiss all of this and insist it is a silly phenomenon, or some unlivable truth, will always feel and hear these words inside, for the rest of these days. And it is not my voice they will hear, not my words. It will be the God within them, addressing what was addressed here. And the voice will become very strong. And when it happens, don't say you've just started channeling; you haven't. And don't say you are hearing a spirit from another dimension; you aren't. And don't say it is your guide; it isn't. It is your God.

Now masters, why has the Ram come back now? Why not one hundred years ago in your counting? Because, although human entities have always gotten into mischief, and you've always been intent on having a lot of peril in your lives, you have always previously managed to somehow get out of it. There have been many raw adventurers in many senses of the word, and you have to have a lot of respect for creatures that are raw adventurers — they are doing something. Well, the lot of you have been raw adventurers in other lives, but you are rather lazy armchair adventurers now. What do you call yourselves? Potatoes on a couch? There is no potato famine in this country! Well, the point is, you never needed so much help before. I've only previously intervened a few times, in historical events that were about to be grossly unfair.

So why now? Because there is an awakening that is occurring

through my outrageous appearance, and more and more people want to hear more and more and more. And they will hear it because the vacuum is closing. There is no room for adventurers in this part of the game; these are the last throes. You have had entities throughout your history who have been brazen, enlightened people, who came to tell you something. You ended up doing away with all of them, more or less. But they all came at various periods in the human drama before a moral collapse and a collapse of the attitudes. And they have been effective most of the time. At least it kept you going.

Now, the end of the world really is not going to happen. Your world could end, according to your attitude. What if you put down this book, walked out your door, and a running hound mashed you flat? Your world, as you know it, would certainly end. It is all a matter of perspective, of course. This Earth is not scheduled to get out of its orbit for quite a while. So, it has a lot of life left, and it is fighting for it. And make no bones about it when I tell you that your auto machines are tearing up the stratosphere. If that hurts you, it should. Because pressing for a better way is how genius occurs; and what allows ingenious individuals to exist in a different vacuum? Creativity! Do you get the drift?

If nothing else changes and everything goes on according to the status quo, there is no need to evolve. If there isn't a reason to have to change how everything is at the present time, nothing will change. And yet, as hard as it has been for you to hear this information, you must realize that this status needs change. And the more of you who are aware of it, the more a consciousness of change exists. Did you ever hear of the old theory of supply and demand? A lot of demanding is going to go on very shortly. And that will create the vacuum for the creators; so it's purposeful, not diresome.

But you have learned a lot. You turned the pages and you have read. That says a great deal about who you are. If there is such a word as disappointment within my understanding of vocabulary, let me say that I have not been disappointed! I revel at your courage; it gladdens me. There is great hope in this readership. Great hope!

So, I came on my father's business and I appeared at a time of critical choice. Because if you continue the spiritual slumber you are in, and you accept the economic conditions that are coming, the vacuum will most certainly collapse on you. And you will have given away the world for it. It was divine intervention to simply allow choice. You can still collapse. But now you have an option, a lot of them. And I desire, from the All that I Am, that you choose wisely what is necessary for your greatest evolution and go for it!

Many of you are familiar with the process through which I give this information, the borrowed body and all that. It has been revolutionary in many ways of understanding applicable personality and demonstrated truth. It is impossible for a person to imitate love. It is impossible for a person to imitate genius. It is impossible to imitate power. And it is impossible to imitate knowingness. It is impossible to imitate all those things unless you are all of those things. And the grand reflection of this is from me to you. All the possibilities are reflected back to you. If you didn't know all of this inside, you couldn't hear it. If you weren't capable of all the love and power, you wouldn't feel it. If you didn't have the genius in you, you couldn't see it in this. That's what this whole performance has been for — for you.

The Last Teaching

There is a last teaching that I will endeavor to communicate in words, and out of this last teaching will come a growing awareness in a few of you of an evolutionary fire. And in this growing fire, a few of you will begin to hear what is not said. And you will hear it clearly. No misinterpretation. No confusion. It is a further advancement into white fire, a higher vibration.

The more you do from the knowledge you have . . . the more your continuum is forever . . . the more open you are . . . the further the physical body evolves. Until finally you become aligned with the Lord God of Your Being and your vibration is attuned, so that you can go forward into the unknown that is unspeakable. And you can know. And you can be empowered.

The last teaching addresses the last limitation. Anything taught hereafter in a public audience will be about the times that are coming and personal perspectives. So, in a sense, it will be a repetition. The rare audiences will come to those who are in the continuum. And that flow will be quite different from what you have experienced in the past with me. And that form will continue till the end of this century. And when I no longer demonstrate through the body physical, I will still be the Ram, the Lord of the Wind, and the power that is alive and vital will be with you, as I have promised. And I will help those of you who make an effort to be helped.

Spiritual charity does not exist. For one who comes into his spirit is not in charity. I'll be with you and I'll help you through these times. But rare will audiences be after this final teaching. By then the word will be recorded, documented, printed, and repeated. It will be visual and historic! And all that you have read and heard in this time will be gathered in the Soul . . . waiting to be lived. What greater thing could I say to you but to say, "Behold, you are God, for the living fire is within you, and all answers pertinent to your path lie within." What greater understanding can I give than to say, "I Am that I Am." And what greater freedom can there be, but to say, "I am my own person."

It has been a long, difficult process, getting you to understand those words; not just read them, but live them! Getting you to understand self, the Lord God of Your Being, encouraging you to glimpse a light that is forever. It has taken all this time . . . all these words . . . to convince you of your divinity and your worthiness. Do you know that many of you insist on being unworthy? Do you know how many of you insist on being victims? You insist because you are too cowardly to take the responsibility for the word victim. Do you know how many of you are gray and conservative and prudish? Let us dare not even utter the number. For the gray are bland and arthritic, and their comings and goings are never noticed, for they make not a ripple on a still pond. I do not speak here of your beautiful, spirited old people, but I speak figuratively, of those who choose to be pale in spirit and action. It has taken you a long time to get to here. Is that something to be ashamed of? It should never be. Never let anyone shame you out of your desire to understand. How long has it taken for you to begin to realize there is a living power within you? Well, if you are starting to realize it, then it has all been worth it. Because, do you know how many powerless lifetimes you've had in seven and a half million years? It was worth it.

And I am not going away. Don't read that into these words. Where would I go? I just Am. And I have never left, no matter what the rumors say. I am just as robust and as colorful. And I am still bordering on temporal vulgarity, as I always have been! But I love you. And every moment you realize something, I rejoice with you. Notice that when you become aware of something, the wind comes up. I want it to come up. I want you to know that you are known. I want you to become aware that there is something aware of you and your precious life. And though the rewards of self-realization are, of themselves, pure, I want you to know that you have a brother, an entity, a lover, a light, that knows when you've made it. And I intend to show you . . . because it brings me grand joy — all of you do.

I am exceedingly pleased with your courage and your ability. And there will come a day when all of this is over and you will toast me in true joy. And that is one toast I will be greatly honored to hear. So be it!

P.S.

I HAVE A P.S. here. Know you a "P.S." — psst? Sort of an afterthought. Be careful of individuals who put on the robe and address the future from what I have said. I do not mean to indict those individuals, but rather their promises. Be careful of offers that promise a large return in a few years. It is one thing for a group to collectively own and go forward in a sharing experience. But remember, each member of a group must contribute to the whole or its strength will be broken.

If you fear the burden of unmerciful taxation coming down on your financial liquidation, do not give your money away in a get-rich-quick scheme. Purchase land with it. There are many people who will need land to work in the Days To Come. And that can add to your tangible worth and will help carry you through.

Purchase small businesses in small towns. Growth in the big cities will be dangerous. There will be a migration, beginning next spring, of people leaving the cities. And those who hold land will gain a reasonable profit. And those who have small businesses will be able to facilitate this for a few years, until the arrival of the debit card. But don't give your money away to someone who is organizing a bank or some similar institution for New Agers. When you depend upon another's singular performance, you are setting yourself up for victimization. Because if their ship doesn't come in, neither will yours; and you will be greatly grieved. Be aware. Don't give anyone anything you can't give freely. If you can't afford to lose it, don't give it!

There are many grand entities who are doers, and they deserve somone taking a chance on them. But they prove themselves in what they do. Do not simply give money away for the purpose of returning a huge barter, because it will not happen. Times are erratic. Don't set yourself up to blame another. It is far greater to lose and know you chose loss, and allow the loss to be there, than to hold blame. Because blame will tie you to all days that are coming. Blame will tie you to victimization, and no matter what you do, you will not gain. It is how reality was created.

It is not worth blaming anyone for anything. I don't care how much you lost. Because what is a bad note compared to seeing the light of all eternity? It should be nothing.

And with your excess monies, buy land and start businesses in places that are small. That is being wise and prudent.

And those of you who have purchased land close to one another, that is wonderful — very smart.

A lot of you are crafty persons? Talented individuals who have what is called craft? You should make it known to one another so that, in the future, you can work through one another. There are many of you who have much to offer; there are many people who need to learn what you know. Make your abilities known somewhere. What do you call them, pages that are yellow? Let's call them "Purple Pages."

In the Northwest you are going to see some erratic gardening. The land of the Great Pacific Northwest is blessed, and becomes more so every day. And for those of you who live elsewhere, if that is where you choose to be because you feel it in your heart — let that land be blessed as well. Just endeavor to get off the zipper! I worry about those of you sitting on its track. There will be another flurry of runners in some densely populated areas very soon, for no pressure has been relieved on the plates.

You might like to know that a few of your brethren who, in recent times, perished in the plagues are now in my kindgom. Contrary to popular belief, they have gone home to the light.

You have read. You have comprehended. I am very pleased. I have nothing more to say to you in regards to that which is termed

Change, The Days To Come, the destiny of man and nature, and personal survival. But *you* have a lot to do. What you have read here will unfold every day for the next twelve years. Unfold with it! That is all! This book is finished. So be it. May the love of God go with you.

Toasts, Prayers, and Manifestations

From The Lord God Of My Being,
unto the glory of God,
unto this day.
Realize my personal need
manifested into life.
And give me the courage to accept it.
To life. Forever, and ever, and ever.
So be it.

From The Lord God Of My Being
unto the glory of God within.
From this moment forward,
into manifested destiny
what give I credence to,
what give I will to,
into the name of God within me,

so it will manifest.
So it will come to pass.
For the glory, and the life, and the forever
of that which is within.

And with that, think about what you want,
because you will get it.

A Final Note from Ramtha:

I LOVE YOU very greatly. And when you determine what those words mean to you and your capacity to understand love, then to the height of that capacity love I you, great masters. You are the hope for new times to come. God surely has blessed you unto the glory of what he is. So be it.

Afterword

Other Books About Ramtha

I Am Ramtha
The first high-quality, full-color photographic and text book on a channeled entity and his teachings. *$24.95 hardcover.*

Ramtha
A beautifully edited and designed collection of the cornerstones of Ramtha's teachings. *$19.95 hardcover.*

A State of Mind, My Story: Ramtha, the Adventure Begins
JZ Knight's moving autobiography in which she tells the story of her life and her involvement with Ramtha. *$15.95 hardcover.*

Becoming, A Master's Manual
Edited by Khit Harding, this book provides a collection of quotes from Ramtha's teachings. *$14.95 quality paperback.*

Destination Freedom: A Time-Travel Adventure
Douglas James Mahr's wonderfully inspiring adventure, under Ramtha's guidance, exploring self-discovery. *$10.95 quality paperback.*

Ramtha Intensive: Soulmates
Transcribed from Ramtha's January 1986 audience on soulmates, love and relationships. *$10.00 quality paperback.*

Ramtha Intensive: Change, The Days to Come
Transcribed from Ramtha's May 1986 audience on man, the environment and what nature has in store. *$10.00 quality paperback.*

Voyage to The New World
A collection of Ramtha's teachings and commentaries written by Douglas James Mahr. *$9.95 quality paperback.*

Manifesting, A Master's Manual
A collection of Ramtha quotes, edited by Khit Harding, to help your understanding of self. *$7.95 quality paperback.*

Upcoming Ramtha Books

Financial Freedom: The Choice
Understanding money, your present conditions and taking control of your financial destiny. *$9.95 quality paperback.*

UFO Raiders From Above
Who they are, where they come from and what they are trying to tell us. *$11.00 quality paperback.*

Other Resource Materials

To experience Ramtha in person, or on audio and video tapes.
Contact Ramtha Dialogues, P.O. Box 1210, Yelm, WA 98597, or call 206-458-5201.

Publisher's Note

Beyond Words Publishing, Inc. produces books of uncompromising standards and integrity, books that invite us to step beyond the limits of our experience to discover what lies within, beyond words.

Our publications include: children's, photographic, nature, self-help, new age and psychology books, as well as calendars and audio tapes.

For a free catalog of our newest titles please contact:

Beyond Words Publishing, Inc.
Pumpkin Ridge Road
Route 3, Box 492-B
Hillsboro, OR 97123
503-647-5109
1-800-284-9673

A celebration of life through publishing.